POWER OF
AFTER

POWER OF AFTER

What's Next Can Be Your Most Purposeful Chapter

DEBORAH JOHNSON

Copyright © 2025 Deborah Johnson

Power of After:
What's Next Can Be Your Most Purposeful Chapter

All rights reserved. No parts of this book may be used or reproduced by any means, graphic, electronic or mechanical, including photocopying, recording, taping or by any information storage retrieval system without the written permission of the publisher except in the case of brief quotations embodied in critical articles and reviews.

Johnson, Deborah, author

Issued in print and electronic format
ISBN: 978-1-7333484-9-2 (hardbound)
ISBN: 978-1-7333484-8-5 (paperback)
ISBN: 979-8-9987217-0-0 (ebook)

Because of the dynamic nature of the internet, any web addresses or links obtained in this book may have changed since publication and may no longer be valid.

Cover design by Deborah Johnson created on ChatGPT
Book design by Wordzworth.com

Deborah's photos by Samir Janjua • Commercial permission

Visit Deborah's websites at DeborahJohnsonSpeaker.com; GoalsForYourLife.com; DJWorksMusic.com

Hero Mountain®, Core Common Denominator®, HALFERS Tool® are Registered Trademarks, All Rights Reserved

For all who find themselves standing at a crossroads, asking, "What's next?" May your next chapter be your most purposeful and fulfilling yet.

Acknowledgements

It's hard to put into words just how much I value the lifelong friends, colleagues, and family who continue to shape and inspire my life. These relationships mean the world to me. You've reminded me to keep learning, keep growing, to laugh more—to take myself a little less seriously. Whether it is laughing and chatting over Pickleball games or walking hills or planning fun outings, my various friends have helped me stay sharp and focused on the bigger picture. Because of those experiences and relationships, I can help others move forward in life and business.

A heartfelt thank you to my dear friend, Paula Miller. Paula, you've been by my side for every writing project, and your editing expertise has been matched only by your genuine friendship. Your honest yet encouraging feedback has meant so much. I'm grateful we share not only a love of words but also many of the same values and perspective on life.

To my family—you are always at the top of my gratitude list. Our sons, Mike, Dan, and Dave, continue to grow in their careers and build beautiful families of their own. What an honor it is to pray for you all—your wives and our amazing grandkids—every day. My hope is that you enjoy your journeys together as much as Greg and I have enjoyed raising you, and that you create memories just as lasting and meaningful.

Finally, to the love of my life, Greg. It's hard to believe how fast the years have gone since we stood together to say, "I do." Every morning cappuccino, every conversation, every quiet moment, and chaotic project—you've been there with love, wisdom, and perspective. I truly couldn't do this without you. In so many ways, I'm rich beyond measure.

Contents

Acknowledgements — vii
Introduction — xv
   Gaining Creative Freedom — xvi
   Purpose of this Book — xvii

PART 1   THE ROLE OF AI IN MODERN BUSINESS

Chapter 1   Understanding AI and Its Impact — 3
   The Growth of AI — 4
   Overcoming the Fear of the Unknown — 5
   Basics of Exponential Growth — 6
   The Role of Input in AI Development — 6

Chapter 2   How AI Enhances, Not Replaces Human Effort — 9
   Demystifying AI: Pulling Back the Curtain — 10
   Types of AI Learning — 12
      Machine learning — 12
      Deep learning — 12
      Generative learning — 13

Chapter 3   AI's Power to Boost Efficiency and Productivity — 15
   AI in Healthcare — 15
   AI in Fraud Detection — 16
   AI for Improved Decision-Making — 17
   Integrating AI into the Workplace — 18

	Where AI Fits into Business	18
	Mastering the Basics Before Diving In	19
	AI in Action: My Experience	20
	Rephrasing and Clarifying	20
	Research	21
	Scheduling and Timelines	22
	Creative Use	23
PART 2	**DESIGNING YOUR IDEAL LIFESTYLE**	
Chapter 4	**A New Business Mindset for a New Era**	27
	Self-Directed Questions	28
	Why Traditional Strategies Need an Update	29
	Blueprint for Success	31
	The Duomo Principle	33
	The Power of Accountability	34
	The Vision of Long-Term Goals	35
	The Strength of Short-Term Goals	36
	Turning Dreams into Reality	37
Chapter 5	**Creating a Purpose-Driven Life**	40
	Regrets, Dreams and "What Ifs"	41
	Setting Age-Proof Goals	42
	The Opportunity to Reinvent Yourself	43
	Defining Core Values and Living by Them	44
	Staying Consistent with Your Values	45
	Defining Your Personal and Professional Truth	46
	Addressing Failures	48
	The Role of Character and Integrity	49
	Guiding Contract for Your Life	50
Chapter 6	**Mastering the Mindset for Success**	52
	Our Brain is Wired for Learning and Change	52
	The Science of Neuroplasticity Growth	54
	The Role of the Prefrontal Cortex in Business Success	55
	How the Hippocampus Influences Decision Making	57
	Prioritizing Health and Wellness	58
	Creating Your Ideal Lifestyle	59

Chapter 7	Application: Creating Your Ideal Lifestyle	61
	Assessment: HALFERS Tool™	61
	Goals: Define and Refine Your Vision	63
	Mindset: Cultivate a Growth-Oriented Perspective	64
	Lifestyle: Design a Life That Aligns with Your Values	65

PART 3   CREATING YOUR IDEAL BUSINESS

Chapter 8	Building a Business with Purpose and Flexibility	69
	Commitment to Your Mission	70
	Developing Mental Flexibility	71
	Overcoming Mental Barriers and Roadblocks	73
	Using Mental Hacks and Shortcuts	74
Chapter 9	Achieving Excellence in Your Work	76
	Commitment with Persistence and Patience	77
	Protecting Your Mindset	78
	The Importance of Evaluation and Assessment	78
	Crafting a Mission Driven Business Model	80
	The Power of Your Story	81
	Passion vs. Expertise—Finding the Balance	82
Chapter 10	Building a Competitive Advantage	84
	Defining Your Unique "Why"	85
	Developing a Competency Bank	85
	Hard vs. Soft Skills—What Matters Most?	87
	Understanding the Market Demand	89
Chapter 11	Positioning Yourself in the Marketplace	91
	Exploring the Heart of Your Purpose	92
	Identifying Your Most Valuable Skills	93
	Crafting a Compelling Selling Proposition	96
Chapter 12	Crafting Simple and Clear Messaging	98
	How to Search for Opportunities	99
	The Power of Repurposing and Diversification	100
	Identifying Your Ideal Customer	101
	Why a Good CRM Matters	103

Chapter 13	Buying Freedom through Smart Financial Decisions	104
	Keeping an Eye on the Money	105
	Understanding Appreciating vs. Depreciating Assets	106
	Conducting Quarterly Business Reviews	107
Chapter 14	Application: Creating Your Ideal Business	109
	To Set Yourself Apart: Four Principles to Apply	109
	One: Define a Unique Strength Based on Your Story	109
	Two: Put Your Transferable Skills into a Repeatable System	110
	Three: Commit to Lifelong Learning and Use Automation	111
	Four: Measure and Adjust for ROI (Return on Investment)	112
	Quick Tips for Financial Health	112
	Core Common Denominator®	113

PART 4   CREATE YOUR AUTOMATION HUB

Chapter 15	Creating a Content and Automation System	119
	Making Automation Work for You	119
	The Importance of a Content Bank	121
	Essential Tools for Business Automation	122
	Password Management System	122
	Website	123
Chapter 16	Building a Strong Online Presence	124
	Website Essentials and Design	125
	Crafting a Clear Business Message	126
	Growing and Managing a Mailing List	128
	Writing Articles for Authority	130
	Creating Social Media Content Strategically	131
Chapter 17	Managing Digital Content Efficiently	133
	Set it Up Right: Save Time Later	133
	Organizing a Creative Content Bank	135
	Structuring a Social Media System	136
	Using a Content Scheduler	137
	Protecting Your Business Assets	140

	Using Project Management Tools and Virtual Assistants	140
Chapter 18	**Leveraging Online Learning Platforms**	**143**
	Third Party e-Learning Platforms	144
	Self-Hosted e-Learning Platforms	145
	Membership Platforms for Recurring Revenue	147
Chapter 19	**Utilizing Video for Business Growth**	**148**
	Choosing the Right Video and Storage Platform	149
	Establishing and Growing Your Video Channel	151
Chapter 20	**Effective Lead Generation Strategies**	**153**
	The Power of Lead Magnets	153
	Hosting Webinars for Engagement	154
	Launching a Podcast to Build Authority	155
Chapter 21	**Writing and Publishing Your Book**	**159**
	Using Books to Expand Your Brand	159
	Understanding Different Book Formats	161
	eBooks	161
	Audiobooks	162
	Print Books	163
Chapter 22	**Closing Comments and Final Applications**	**165**
	If It Sounds Too Good, It Might Be	165
	How I Choose and Use New Virtual Tools	166
	My Evaluation Process	166
	Example: Video and Livestreaming	166
	Testing and Making a Decision	167
	Reflection and Next Steps	167
	Applying What You've Learned	168
Quotes		169
About the Author		171
Resources		173
Endnotes		175

Introduction

The afternoon forecast called for rain, but when I stepped out for my early-morning five-mile walk, only a light mist appeared—no real rain. It was chilly, so I bundled up in gloves and my warm, fuzzy, black jacket, the one without a hood. Our little dog, Amelia, wore her red coat and pranced happily beside me. By the time we reached the third hill, the mist had thickened to a fog. Soon, it turned to a steady drizzle; in ten minutes more, it became a full-on rain, a real downpour.

Returning home, the entry mirror reflected my soggy misery: dripping hair plastered my head; my warm, fuzzy jacket resembled the soggy fur of a wet, black dog. Little Amelia kept shaking to dry her dripping fur. Why had I not worn my hooded raincoat? It would have saved me much time as I prepared for my work day. Those phone weather app predictions are not always reliable. I should have known better, but I was caught unprepared.

In the same way, many are unprepared for the expansion of AI.

It's here. The drizzling sprinkle of innovation has become a steady rain turning into a storm. We can be prepared, not with the knowledge about every single aspect of AI, but with its basic premises. This knowledge will demystify some of its power and capabilities and dispel some fear and anxiety of its exponential growth. It's time to put on the raincoat of knowledge. Unless we do, we will find ourselves feeling like a big, wet dog caught in the rain, unprepared.

Gaining Creative Freedom

It has taken me years to craft a method for doing business that incorporates the entrepreneurial creative freedom that I love with a business engine that can run with or without me. I have received a boatload of advice, along with many promotional offers from "experts." Some proved valuable while many others did not fit my situation.

When arriving at the halftime of my life, I wanted to expand my business and influence while still fulfilling my love for creating. I had already written and produced a volume of music and was continually releasing songs for licensing and purchase. However, I felt I could make more impact by helping others succeed. As I added speaking to my skills, I found I had entered another performance field beyond professional musician and composer. This new arena held additional options for creating a platform of influence, not just products.

Writing books, crafting articles, growing my newsletter, creating online courses, and starting a podcast became utensils I added to my professional toolkit. My training and experience provided a solid groundwork for acquiring further skills. The number of projects I had produced in my small recording studio provided many opportunities for problem solving. Anyone who has produced albums and musicals understands the work and tenacity it takes to successfully release projects and launch events.

My teaching career began at age thirteen when I taught piano to neighborhood kids and their parents. At first, I discounted this skill as being less important than a musical career where I performed for large audiences. However, the ability to break down tasks and impart knowledge to others has provided a foundation for my business landscape, enhanced by technical expertise and amplified by certain life skills. I've enjoyed this process more and more as I've applied this adaptive skill to many virtual, as well as live settings.

I have spoken with many who desire professional change, especially at midcareer. How can they create a lifestyle they love? For some, this means running their own businesses. Yet they are afraid a business will soon "own them," by requiring demanding hours and great energy. Some want to focus on more travel or to fulfil a bucket list. Then, others want to serve in organizations that give back, to make a difference; however, they are stymied by time and energy constraints. Further, many possess a fear of technology, especially with the growth of AI. They are out of touch and often left behind, confused about doing business with technology and automation. AI has now become the villain that threatens the way they have always lived or run their businesses.

Purpose of this Book

Part of my purpose in writing this book is to simplify the principles behind AI, to make it easier to understand by dispelling some of the fear. AI is here to stay, so understanding its basic principles will help us navigate its uses, as well as understand its scope. Automation is supercharged with some of the capabilities of AI, but it's important for users to be in control, to understand its power. I have spent many hours struggling with tech issues in the past. In the struggle, I have discovered wonderful shortcuts and systems that not only mitigate the time involved in running a business but also free up space for "living." Activities such as traveling, spending time with my family, working remotely and managing a team from anywhere in the world comprise my focus at this time. I describe some of my system in this book but fully expect readers to develop their own. Many are looking forward to retiring but still want to keep skills sharp and use the experiences they've gathered through the years. They just don't know how or what area to pursue.

I hope the *Power of After* encourages you to move ahead, to affirm your background and experience so that you can significantly plan your next chapter. Our world needs experienced, values-focused voices that can encourage and influence upcoming generations. With medical advances and greater life expectancies, these "midlife years" can be the best, most significant years of your life. If you are already moving forward with plans, my hope is you will discover some additional tools to successfully manage not only your business, but also your life.

First, I will briefly approach the basics of AI to dispel the fear surrounding its use and development. We are still in control. Disclaimer: this book wasn't written by AI. I wrote it based on principles I've created and taught. However, I've used AI tools for editing, research and expansion, always verifying sources.

Our civilization has been built on technology from the invention of the wheel to written language to electricity and to the internet. Embracing changing technology, then using it, is powerful. Look around you. Your lights turn on with a switch or command; you quickly scan items at the grocery self-checkout; you press a button to make an online order, then have products delivered to your front door, overnight. All this happens because of technology and the power of AI. It need not be overwhelming. So if you've been on the fence, waiting to take your next steps forward, this book is for you.

PART ONE

The Role of AI in Modern Business

CHAPTER ONE

Understanding AI and Its Impact

*Once there is a simple understanding of the basic
way AI works, the fear will disintegrate.*

The small white cylinder kept its shape at the bottom of the shower. The warm water flowed directly on the essential oils steamer, as I waited to breathe in its calming peppermint aroma. Yet no matter how deeply I inhaled, I could detect no sweet smell. Interestingly, the cylinder remained undissolved. Was it a multiple-use disc, I wondered. That would certainly be a cost-effective product.

After my second aroma-less shower, I noticed that the cylinder still had its clear sealed packaging intact. That explained why the aromatic disc had not immediately disintegrated under the warm water. It's plastic coating kept its aroma locked inside. If I had not examined it, who knows how many showers I would have taken without the benefits of the oil disc's aromatic contents.

In many ways, a coating of mystery surrounds much about artificial intelligence (AI). Until the outer coating is peeled away, AI's power will remain locked inside. However, once users gain a simple understanding of the way AI works, the fear and resistance will disintegrate, just like an essential oil shower disk. I hope to unwrap some of that coating in this section of the book.

The Growth of AI

Remember the Pee-Chee? Most baby boomers probably recall it well. I carried the yellow folder with the one-to-twelve multiplication tables to school for quickly completing simple math equations. Then, an amazing tool called the *calculator* replaced the Pee-Chee. It allowed me to enter numbers on a small electronic keypad then, poof! The equation's solution would appear on a tiny screen. The calculators did not erode people's math ability as some feared. It just made doing math more efficient.

The simple calculator evolved into advanced machines that could solve formulas for engineering, medical use, and other fields. Today, when we access a calculator, we automatically assume that it will provide the requested information. We never question *how* it works, only that it *does* work, saving us time and mental energy. Everyone can use a simple calculator with its basic commands without any fear of technology.

With the advent of the internet, world wide web, and search bars, answers and connection times grew faster and more powerful. Today, dial-up connections have given way to links by satellite, fiber optics, cellular networks, and hotspots. We need not question *how* a search engine works; we merely expect that it *will* work. If we want to find *how* it works, we can search the internet for additional information that multiplies daily. In 2024, approximately 252,000 new websites were created each day, contributing to over 1.1 billion websites online.[1] All of this data is available for search engines like Google to crawl and index as it's continuously updated.

Overcoming the Fear of the Unknown

AI, however, feels different. We have many questions: *How does it work? How do I use it? What if I'm confused?* or *Will AI make my job obsolete?* Movies about robots with expressionless faces, marching in unison, overtaking everything in their path do appear frightening! The power of technology certainly raises valid questions that deserve an answer. Yet we can use AI's power to fuel and expand the tools we need. We can use it effectively, setting parameters that deliver the most accurate information. I can show you how.

I will start by unwrapping that coating of mystery enveloping AI and its power. New programs and tools are released by the minute. However, the basic principles of the creation of those tools and their growth are the same. If we understand *how* AI. works, we can make decisions on the best programs and systems needed to unlock its potential.

After we cover the basics of AI, we will move to sections two and three that cover creating one's ideal lifestyle and business before approaching automation. I encourage readers to explore all sections, as the principles covered in sections two and three provide important context for understanding and applying AI alongside automation in section four.

Basics of Exponential Growth

If someone establishes a bank account at a very young age and keeps putting money in it, his account will grow, as the compound interest multiplies his small investment. For example, investing $50 annually from age five to twenty results in total contributions of $800 over sixteen years. Assuming an annual interest rate of 2%, compounded annually, by age fifty you'd have $3,594.64 and age eighty, $8,539.59.

Compound interest is a specific example of exponential growth. When interest is added to the principal, and future interest calculations include this accumulated interest, the investment grows exponentially. This multiplication principle is similar to the way AI propagates, by building on its own growth like compound interest, only faster. This type of speed can be frightening, but we should not be alarmed.

The Role of Input in AI Development

When memorizing a spelling list, we reinforce each word through repetition and practice. Those words then reside in our brain's memory to be retrieved when writing or speaking. In a similar way, all AI models are trained on the input and storage of large databases. That information is then retrieved for content generation. Both processes involve recognizing and internalizing patterns; a human learns the sequence of letters in words while AI learns patterns in data. Repetition enhances proficiency in both spelling and AI output.

Input is crucial for growth and effectiveness of AI, directly influencing the learning process and outcome. The quality and quantity of data fed into AI models are foundational to their development. For example, machine learning models learn from vast datasets, and the more diverse, accurate, and relevant the input data is, the better AI can perform. Over the years, significant data have been used to train AI systems, with billions of data points processed from various sources like social media, healthcare records, and customer behavior.

The statistic that over 2.5 quintillion bytes of data are created daily is widely cited across various sources, including Forbes[2], providing a constant flow of input for AI models. As these data continue to grow, so too does the potential of AI to improve decision-making, automate tasks, and even predict future trends. It's important to note that data generation rates are continually increasing, with estimates suggesting that by 2025, the amount of data generated each day will reach 463 exabytes globally.[3]

The magnitude of those numbers makes my head spin, so I asked ChatGPT to make this easier to understand:

2.5 quintillion bytes created daily is:

- 2,500,000 terabytes (TB) or
- 2,500,000,000 gigabytes (GB).

This data range is equivalent to hundreds of millions of hours of HD video, all being generated globally in a single day!

463 exabytes (EB) of data by 2025 is equivalent to:

- 463,000 petabytes (PB), or
- 463,000,000 terabytes (TB), or
- 463,000,000,000 gigabytes (GB).

The ability to access that data quickly and easily, then build on it is the beauty of AI as a tool. To use calculators to get the same numbers I just shared would take a great deal of time while the answer comes immediately from ChatGPT. The machines will continue to automate complex tasks to learn and generate more content based on input. Also, the quality of input is important to the outcome. This will be an important principle as we use AI in our own lives and businesses.

CHAPTER TWO

How AI Enhances, Not Replaces Human Effort

*Think of AI as an opportunity to grow
and innovate at your own pace.*

Tools using AI and automation don't have to be intimidating; in fact, they can be empowering when approached with the right mindset. Those tools are designed to assist, not replace, human efforts. They have the power to make daily tasks more efficient, freeing up time for creativity and strategic thinking. Just as we once learned to navigate email or smartphones, learning to use AI is a step-by-step process that becomes easier with practice. The key is to start small. We can first experiment with one tool or feature that addresses a specific need in our business or life. As we gain familiarity, we'll discover that these tools are not overwhelming but serve as allies, making our work more manageable and effective. AI provides opportunity for us to grow and innovate at our own pace.

Millennium Falcon: Smugglers Run is an interactive motion simulator attraction located in Star Wars: Galaxy's Edge at Disneyland Park in Anaheim, California. The experience lasts approximately four and a half minutes. The first time that I sat in one of the six simulator seats, I was unprepared for the intense visuals, loud audio, and jerky movements. Even though I knew it was just a simulator, it felt real, and I felt out of control. My stomach was turning in circles as I stumblingly exited the Corellian light freighter.

Though I have never experienced light speed in real life, the Disney simulator helped me imagine its power and potential. That experience helps me to visualize the speed of AI. It can automate repetitive tasks, streamline workflows, and provide data-driven insights like the speed of light, allowing businesses to operate more efficiently and focus on strategic activities. Harnessing that power is to our advantage.

Demystifying AI: Pulling Back the Curtain

In *The Wizard of Oz*, when Dorothy and her friends finally meet the Wizard, they face a terrifying display—an enormous head, a ball of fire, and fearsome sounds. However, Dorothy's dog, Toto, pulls back a curtain to reveal that these spectacles are the work of an ordinary man operating machinery and speaking into a microphone. This man, who had been presenting himself as the powerful Wizard of OZ, is a regular person, using tricks to maintain an illusion of grandeur.

Even though AI is not merely an illusion, I'll pull back the curtain on how AI works and the differences between machine and generative learning. Because AI is already being used to tackle complex challenges and improve efficiency in a variety of industries, understanding where it's being used and the different types of outcomes helps to dispel some of its mystery.

Artificial Intelligence focuses on performing tasks that typically require human intelligence. It causes us to imagine the possibilities if we didn't have human limitations, achieving super-human status. Currently, AI doesn't have the human ability to fully reason or feel emotion, but AI systems are designed to learn from experience, then constantly improve. Some learning takes place without reinforcement while some requires reinforcement.

Types of AI Learning

Machine learning

Machine learning is a branch of artificial intelligence (AI) that enables computers to learn and improve from experience without being explicitly programmed. It uses algorithms to analyze large amounts of data, identify patterns, and make predictions or decisions based on that data. Imagine a huge Excel document containing much data. The organized and structured data are then used for AI analysis and outcome.

For example, machine learning powers recommendations on *streaming platforms, fraud detection in banking, and voice recognition in virtual assistants.* Machine learning continually adapts and improves as it processes more organized data to solve complex problems and automate tasks in diverse industries. In fields of finance or medicine, machine learning is extremely useful in performing calculations and determining patterns. The information doesn't make decisions for us, but provides the tools to make better decisions.

Deep learning

Deep learning is a type of AI that trains computers to learn and make decisions by recognizing unorganized patterns in large amounts of data. Imagine large amounts of data in no particular order, then gathered for analysis. Deep learning works like a human brain by using **layers of artificial neurons** to process distributed bits of information, improving its accuracy over time without needing to be explicitly programmed. This technology is behind tools like *voice assistants, facial recognition, self-driving cars, and language translation.*

Generative learning

Generative learning is a subset of machine learning focused on creating *new data* that resembles the original data it was trained on. Unlike traditional machine learning models that focus on predictions or classifications, generative learning **creates something entirely new** by learning patterns and structures from existing datasets. For example, creative illustrations for articles can be created with *Canva's* software version of generative learning. Some illustrations I've created using *Canva* are suitable for use, while others are not—this is also true for illustrations generated by platforms like ChatGPT and others, which use generative learning models. Generative learning has immense potential for creativity, design, and innovation across industries, enabling businesses to automate creative processes or develop unique solutions tailored to their needs.

It is not necessary to understand the inner-workings of machine learning and generative learning to effectively use AI. However, when ChatGPT asks us what version of an answer we like best, that's machine learning at work to create content that aligns with our style or preferences. When telling a generative learning tool like DALL-E about a specific design we'd like to create, it will create a new image, or even several new images from which to choose based on your responses. And it's done extremely fast.

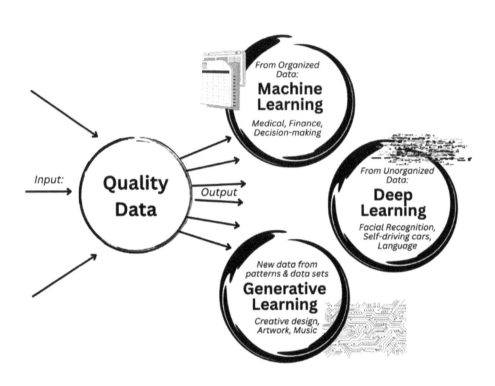

CHAPTER THREE

AI's Power to Boost Efficiency and Productivity

The possibilities for AI applications span nearly every industry, offering transformative potential.

AI can automate repetitive tasks, streamline workflows, and provide data-driven insights, allowing businesses to operate more efficiently and focus on strategic activities. Below are some examples for healthcare and fraud detection using machine learning.

AI in Healthcare

AI is especially valuable in early disease identification. This area is growing quickly. Soon there will be tests for some conditions that stay hidden until it's too late for treatment, such as *cervical cancer* or the diagnosis of abnormalities in image recognition.[4] The

American Cancer Society estimates that in the United States in 2025, 13,360 new cases of invasive cervical cancer will be diagnosed and about 4,320 deaths.[5] It's the fourth most common cancer in women globally, so these statistics underscore the importance of regular screenings and preventative healthcare.

Lauren Bannon, a mother of two, was diagnosed with rheumatoid arthritis after four months of testing, despite negative results for the condition. Her symptoms began in February 2024 with stiff fingers and severe stomach pain, leading to a 14-pound weight loss in a month—initially blamed on acid reflux. In a desperate move, she turned to ChatGPT, which suggested Hashimoto's disease, an autoimmune disorder targeting the thyroid. After pressing doctors to test for it, they were surprised to find ChatGPT was right. Further tests revealed two small lumps in her neck, confirmed as cancer in October 2024. Bannon believes ChatGPT helped uncover what might have otherwise gone undiagnosed due to her atypical symptoms with no family history of Hashimoto's disease, consequently saving her life.[6]

Healthcare currently uses AI to analyze patient data and medical literature to provide doctors with evidence-based treatment options. Data that used to take months and even years to analyze is now performed immediately, allowing researchers to build upon that data. This area will continue to grow.

AI in Fraud Detection

In finance, AI has become a pivotal tool in detecting fraudulent activities. When deviations of normal patterns occur, the system flags them by analyzing data. This is why we receive notices to approve a purchase if it falls outside our normal purchasing pattern. I have received notifications while traveling when the vendor isn't easily identified.

It can be annoying when a transaction doesn't go through promptly, but ultimately, it will save both the card holder and the company time and resources. It's additionally frustrating when my card is cancelled as it takes time to go back through every automated payment to update my card. However, I know the protections are in my best interest.

AI also excels in detecting new and evolving fraud tactics by recognizing subtle anomalies that rule-based systems might miss. For example, PayPal[7] uses AI and deep learning to analyze billions of transactions, helping it detect fraud with high accuracy and results in significantly reducing false positives.

AI for Improved Decision-Making

By analyzing large datasets, AI helps businesses make informed decisions, predict market trends, and understand customer behavior. This leads to better strategic planning. The key is the ability to analyze large amounts of data quickly. This is an area where more and more programs and services are available every day to help businesses, both large and small.

For example, I can see how many people access and download my podcast from different countries around the world. I also have a program that lets me see who has visited my website and the pages they've accessed and even how long they have stayed on those pages. Since I have large websites, it helps me to check webpages often to make sure they load quickly and contain all the most current information with links that are live and working correctly.

Integrating AI into the Workplace

Most of us notice, when searching for an item on Amazon, that the website includes at least five more suggestions of additional products based on what was last viewed. This is basic AI at work. We also see some of the same suggestions pop up on our social media feeds. It is because of cookies, which are small text files that websites store on our devices during browsing sessions. Cookies remember our preferences. We have the ability to clear browsing data by accessing our history, but most of us don't bother.

Nearly every business, knowingly or unknowingly, is already leveraging AI in some capacity. While AI has existed for years, its evolution—particularly in the areas of generative capabilities and machine learning—has amplified its power by harnessing vast knowledge bases and unprecedented speed. The possibilities for AI applications span nearly every industry, offering transformative potential.

Where AI Fits into Business

The *Heineken Company*, which has been in business over 150 years, calls itself the "World's most international brewer." It is family owned and consistently uses AI. In an interview with chief technology and digital officer Ronald den Elzen[8], he explained how Heineken uses AI extensively in revenue management and optimization of promotions. However, he believes much of the value of using AI comes from predictive analytics to find patterns for educated guesses about future trends based on historical data. The combination of both machine and generative learning helps the company forge ahead with innovation that's based on data with power to minimize mistakes.

As consumers of AI tools, the challenge lies in staying open to learning and strategically adopting tools that align with specific business needs. The key is to focus on solutions that provide the greatest value relative to the time and energy required for implementation. By making thoughtful choices, businesses can capitalize on AI's capabilities while ensuring it serves their unique goals effectively.

Mastering the Basics Before Diving In

I'm not sure how much additional preparation would have helped me in high school swimming when facing the high dive, but I like to think it would have alleviated some of the pain. I still remember the fear of standing on the edge of that high platform, wearing the required baggy, yellow one-piece bathing suit, trembling as I performed four perfectly executed bellyflops. I'm happy to say that I finally passed with a far-from-perfect dive but have never attempted a similar dive since that fateful day.

Before diving into automation, technology, and AI, it's essential to first prepare by establishing a solid business foundation, guided by business intelligence, market trends, and demand. This foundation should also align with a person's ideal lifestyle and business goals.

Many people make the mistake of stepping right out on the high dive before first defining their ideal lifestyle—one that reflects their core values and growth mindset. Then, when building a purpose-driven business around that lifestyle, automation and AI become easier to integrate and significantly more effective. With this strong foundation in place, one can dive in with confidence.

AI in Action: My Experience

In this section, I'll share a few basic examples of how AI is currently being used. I'll primarily focus on *ChatGPT*—a widely available and free tool. While the free version offers plenty of functionality, it does have limitations. Like many digital tools, more advanced features are available with a subscription. To get started with a free account, simply visit *chatgpt.com*.[9]

Rephrasing and Clarifying

ChatGPT can help rewrite or refine language to make our messages clearer, more engaging, or better suited to a specific audience or tone. I often use ChatGPT to help rephrase or simplify sections of text I've written.

> *As an example, here was my prompt:*
> Rephrase this for clarity: The written word continues to hold value, especially for a creator of content and intellectual property. Also, there are many who feel they'd like to document family history to help and encourage future generations. Writing memoirs is a great vehicle to provide a record to be carried forward.
>
> *Here is the reply from ChatGPT:*
> The written word remains highly valuable, particularly for those who create content and intellectual property. Many people also feel compelled to document their family history as a way to inspire and guide future generations. Writing memoirs serves as an excellent means to preserve these stories, ensuring they are passed down and remembered.

Research

ChatGPT can quickly summarize complex topics, provide definitions, or offer context, helping one gather ideas or background information efficiently. Creating a clear and specific prompt is crucial when using a virtual tool like ChatGPT because it guides the tool to deliver more accurate, relevant, and useful responses.

Here is a prompt asking for a source:

What are the dates of Aristotle's works? Give a source:

Here is the reply from ChatGPT:

Aristotle (384–322 BCE) authored numerous works across diverse subjects, including philosophy, science, and politics. While the exact dates of composition for many of his writings are uncertain, scholars have made educated estimates based on historical context and Aristotle's life events. Here's an overview of some of his notable works and their approximate dates:

Early Works (circa 367–347 BCE) – During his time at Plato's Academy: *World History Encyclopedia*

Protrepticus (Exhortation to Philosophy) – An early work encouraging the pursuit of philosophy.

Eudemus – A dialogue reflecting Platonic themes.

Middle Period (circa 347–335 BCE) – After leaving the Academy and during his travels:

Topics – Discusses dialectical reasoning.

On Sophistical Refutations – Examines logical fallacies.

Later Works (circa 335–322 BCE) – During his time at the Lyceum in Athens:

> *Nicomachean Ethics* – Explores moral philosophy. *Internet Encyclopedia of Philosophy*
>
> *Politics* – Analyzes political theory and practice.
>
> *Metaphysics* – Investigates the nature of being and reality.
>
> *Physics* – Studies the principles of natural phenomena.
>
> *Poetics* – Focuses on literary theory, especially tragedy.

It's important to note that many of Aristotle's works were likely edited and compiled by his students after his death, which adds to the uncertainty regarding their exact dates of composition.

It is important to verify sources, as some may be unreliable or contain inaccurate information. Many sources may not be viable or may contain information that is inaccurate. For example, three different sources were listed for Aristotle, including the *World History Encyclopedia* and *Wikipedia*.[10]

Scheduling and Timelines

We can use ChatGPT to outline a step-by-step plan or timeline for projects, launches, or content calendars, breaking big tasks into manageable steps. I asked ChatGPT to provide the following information for a new book release: Give me the steps that should be taken in the first month of a new book release. Create a timeline with a daily "to do" list of small steps. I received the answer in two forms.

The first was a list of a first month release timeline daily "to-do list" with Day 1, Day 2, etc. Then, I was asked, *Would you like this as a printable checklist or content calendar PDF?* I requested the PDF and received a link to download a three-page PDF. Personally, I liked the daily "to-do list" better than the PDF, but the PDF would have been easily revised with another prompt.

Creative Use

ChatGPT can help generate visuals—like concept illustrations, promotional graphics, or even pencil sketch-style artwork—by transforming descriptions or photos into custom images that match one's vision. Several illustrations in this book were created using ChatGPT, including pencil sketches made from my photos—like the *Londolozi* images in Chapter Eight taken from my trip to South Africa.

The more we use tools like ChatGPT, the better they reflect our voices. While upgrades are available, the free version is often sufficient for most users.

PART TWO

Designing Your Ideal Lifestyle

CHAPTER FOUR

A New Business Mindset for a New Era

Strike a balance between the freedom you long for and the fulfillment that comes from using your expertise to make a difference and give back.

Ellie couldn't wait to retire. She had a long list of projects that she was eager to finally tackle. She wanted to organize her travel photos into albums to enjoy the memories for years to come. Unfinished home improvement projects awaited her attention, and she wanted time to visit friends she hadn't seen in years. After decades of hard work, she had earned some well-deserved leisure time. Yet questions loomed: Could she afford to stop working? More importantly, would she be happy?

Because inflation had increased the cost of nearly everything, especially food, Ellie questioned if her savings fund was enough to sustain her for the years ahead. Further, she liked staying busy. After completing her first round of projects, would she be bored? She couldn't imagine herself with nothing to do. If her friends were still working, when could they meet? She didn't want to spend evenings alone or constantly bug her friends to get together.

Self-Directed Questions

Many of us ask the same questions as Ellie. Today, there's no set retirement age, and for many, full retirement isn't as appealing as it once was. Relaxing on a beach reading a novel sounds nice, and pickleball will help us stay active—but there has to be more. We've spent years building valuable skills and experience that are still in demand, even if we occasionally feel outdated. The key is to find balance between the freedom we desire and the fulfillment of using our expertise to make an impact and give back. This book offers ideas for shaping work that fits various lifestyles—allowing time for family, travel, and personal projects—perhaps even building on what one is already doing, but on her terms.

Work remains an important part of our human existence as it gives us dignity and purpose. Even Pope John Paul II's 1981 *Laborem Exercens*[11] affirmed this concept, as his words were taken straight from the canonical scriptures "fill the earth and subdue it." (Genesis 1:28) The type and volume of work we seek is our choice, especially at mid-career or the halftime of life.

In today's fast-evolving business landscape, while the fundamentals remain timeless, advancements in technology, the rise of remote work, and global opportunities are reshaping how we operate in a *New*

Way of Doing Business. Yet, amid this transformation, our core values stand as the bedrock of integrity, guiding us in navigating this new era of business. In this section, we explore the need for a fresh approach to business and the work to which we aspire, while highlighting why core foundational principles are more important than ever.

I am writing this, not as one in my 20s, 30s or even 40s. Unlike Ellie, I am fully in the second half of my life. There are many, just like me, who don't want to completely quit working. Professionals like me still want to create impact and plan work around a desired lifestyle. In my experience, I maintained my expertise as a musician, then expanded my reach to include writing, speaking, and podcasting. It has been fun, challenging and incredibly rewarding because I love helping others achieve their dreams by leveraging their experience, common sense, and skills in ways that bring the most fulfillment. After years of refining an automation system for my own business, I've developed a transferable, customizable approach, which I outline in the final section of this book as a guide. Embracing technology doesn't require advanced technical skills—today's tools make it easier than ever for non-tech-minded individuals to harness its potential. This system also incorporates essential goal-setting principles and foundational business strategies to set others up for success.

Why Traditional Strategies Need an Update

The integration of new technologies like AI, automation and advanced software has fundamentally transformed traditional business practices. These tools offer unprecedented capabilities to collect data not only for lightning-fast analyzation but also to predict behavior. Whether the situation involves an entrepreneur, small business, or scalable large business, AI helps to track and engage clients, streamline operations, and enhance efficiency.

However, with these advancements comes a significant shift from "old school" methods, necessitating different strategies to effectively implement and leverage emerging technologies. In some cases, however, new tech tools that promise to simplify life and grow a business only bring frustration because they are ineffective. I've had my share of frustrating tech issues. For example, I've shut my website down after adding some new plugin that conflicted with my software. Furthermore, I have faced major hacks, causing computer and website havoc. These frustrating events waste valuable time. From these disasters, I know that a good system is not only helpful, but essential, providing business professionals with knowledge to harness tools that align with the core principles of business management as well as life management.

It's no longer okay to just say, "I'm not good at tech." Rather, we all need to say, "We can manage tech." A willingness to learn is crucial despite the frustration that such new experience brings. For those of us who have competed in sports, music or other areas, we understand the commitment that is required to become better, faster, or more competent. This is the required mindset for those who adopt AI since it is now embedded in many routine processes.

Creating a structured plan that balances the adoption of new tools with the preservation of core business values ensures that *technology serves the business*, not the other way around, and helps professionals avoid the pitfalls of overextension and distraction.

Regular evaluation of tools and strategies, aligned with core values and goals is key to maintaining focus and achieving long-term success.

There are basics steps that relate specifically to our mindsets at the halftime of life and will influence how we approach the future when using current tools and basic automation. We start with goals.

Blueprint for Success

Letting go of the ladder wasn't easy. It had belonged to my father, so every time I used it to pick fruit from our trees, it reminded me of him. However, the old wooden ladder had become unsteady, and each time I climbed it, I gripped a sturdy branch—just in case it gave out.

I finally ordered a new ladder, which I now love and use regularly. Why did it take me so long to let go of that rickety old ladder? Ultimately, I had to overcome my emotional attachment to that ladder and its sentimental value. My experience reflects a common struggle. We cling to old habits, possessions, or ideals long past their usefulness. In the same way, our past goals may need updating or reimagining, as we navigate a future with shifting priorities and uncertainties.

Goals often get a bad reputation because they are unrealistic. Sometimes, the prospect of setting new goals feels overwhelming or intimidating. Often, we hesitate to set goals at halftime because we fear failure, commitment, change or even success. For some, past setbacks have left them doubting their ability to follow through. I've known many who delay taking the next step—whether in a career shift, business move, or financial goal—because past disappointments drained their confidence. This hesitation can become a habit of resistance and procrastination, yet the underlying desire for positive change remains.

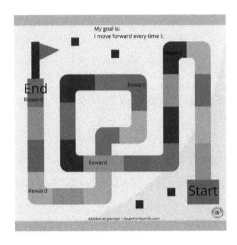

Goals are not just wishful thinking but essential blueprints for success. Whether in life or business, goals provide clarity and direction. They act as guiding stars, helping us navigate the chaos of daily distractions and focus on the important. Without targeted goals, our efforts can feel scattered, leaving us feeling unfulfilled or lost. Goals give purpose, structure, and progress, allowing us to measure growth and celebrate achievements.

The key to achieving goals lies in the approach. Ambitious goals without a clear plan lead to frustration or burnout. Most can identify with feelings of defeat and the mild depression resulting from missed opportunities. To combat the procrastination habit and delaying dreams, it is helpful to break goals into tiny, manageable steps instead of leaping into overwhelming tasks. This step-by-step approach allows us to build momentum while celebrating small victories. Each small achievement reinforces our confidence and creates a sense of progress, making even the most daunting objectives feel achievable. Even if we feel like we've heard such advice before, it is vital to keep reading and most importantly, start applying wise, strategic principles.

The Duomo Principle

Climbing to the top of the **Duomo in Florence, Italy** involves ascending 463 narrow, winding steps through steep corridors and tight passageways, offering glimpses of stunning frescoes on the interior of Brunelleschi's dome. As visitors climb higher, they navigate through ancient stone staircases and small lookout points until reaching the top, where a breathtaking 360-degree panoramic view of Florence awaits. I made reservations on our trip to Florence to climb to the top.

After being admitted through a small side door, we received a clear warning—after the halfway point, there was no turning back. As we climbed the steep, narrow steps. I managed just fine with my size 6½ shoes, but my husband with his size 14 feet barely fit on each step. He turned back at the halfway mark while I continued, motivated by a desire to behold the spectacular view from the top. As I rounded a steep turn, I observed a woman huddled in the corner, trembling. My heart skipped a beat, fearing she might be having a heart attack. Through sobs, she confessed to having a panic attack.

I quickly encouraged her to take deep breaths. She complied, but still her body trembled. She explained that her group had gone on without her. Pushing aside my disgust at her having been abandoned by her companions, I offered to help her reach the top. I calmly explained that if she would hold my hand, we could climb together. Hesitantly, she agreed, and together, we ascended one steep step at a time with one hand in mine and the other on the rail. After several shaky pauses, she finally reached the top. The experience served as a powerful reminder: everyone needs a good guide. Many individuals are unsure of their next steps.so they huddle in fear instead of moving forward.

The Power of Accountability

For many years, I taught voice and piano to private students, holding them accountable for what we covered the previous week and preparing them for performance. Every student not only learned and achieved their goals, but also improved their performance. When a student put in the work, the return on investment was always substantial. Achieving a set goal rests on the value of accountability. The average return on investment (ROI) from hiring a coach is seven times the cost according to a global survey by *Price Waterhouse Cooper* and the *Association Resource Center*[12].

This is why teams employ athletic coaches, who set extremely strict guidelines for players so that they ultimately obtain the desired results. With varying leadership styles, these guides aim to toughen up their players. For example, my husband worked under a baseball coach who pushed his team to win the College World Series. The coach used different methods than most, but still his team did well when pushed to excellence. Thus, consistent accountability, including self-accountability, when implemented and followed, still leads to results. The principle applies to areas of personal development and business plans as well as competitive sports or competitions.

The Vision of Long-Term Goals

Over the years, my long-term goals have consisted of producing albums, musicals, books and online courses. To succeed, I set a proposed end date for the completion of each project. Long-term goals are the milestones that define aspirations for the future, typically stretching over months to years. These goals provide a purpose and direction—a guiding force, fueling daily decisions and efforts. Whether it's achieving career milestones, building a business, earning a degree, or creating a fulfilling personal life, long-term goals give shape to the lives we want to create.

Long-term goals are powerful because they inspire and challenge us to think bigger. They encourage planning, perseverance, and discipline, stretching us beyond comfort zones moving toward the meaningful. However, long-term goals require patience and consistent effort. Breaking them into smaller, actionable steps with short-term goals makes them attainable; tracking progress over time keeps motivation alive. With a clear vision and commitment, long-term goals become a roadmap for success and fulfillment.

The Strength of Short-Term Goals

I divide each of my long-term goals into small steps, which helps me stay on task with the many revisions that are required until completion. Short-term goals are the building blocks of long-term success. These are objectives designed to be achieved within a relatively short timeframe, ranging from a day to a few months. Unlike lofty, distant aspirations, short-term goals are immediate and actionable, providing a sense of focus and direction in the here and now. They keep us motivated and engaged.

A significant benefit of short-term goals is building momentum. Accomplishing a tangible objective—like completing a chapter of a book, organizing a workspace, or making the first call in a sales strategy—provides a quick win to confidence and encourage further action. We can adjust short-term goals as we refine our approaches, learn from each step and steadily improve. For example, with recording projects, I kept a progress sheet, listing each selection on an album project. Every piece would have updates to be made at the next session. These smaller goals created a feedback loop of achievement and momentum.

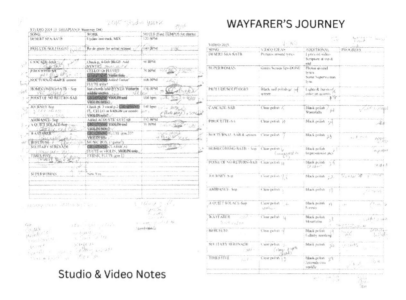

Studio & Video Notes

Employing this strategy has allowed me to finish many projects. To demonstrate, I've included a scan of my studio sheets and video outline for the project "Wayfarer's Journey," an instrumental album of twelve original compositions. I broke large projects into small steps, then each completed step built moved the project forward. This principle applies to almost any project. Small steps make larger tasks easier. The process of completion creates momentum that builds on momentum.

Turning Dreams into Reality

Short-term and long-term goals are like two sides of the same coin, turning dreams into reality. While long-term goals provide the vision and ultimate destination, short-term goals serve as the actionable steps toward that vision. The two are interdependent—long-term goals give meaning and context to your short-term efforts while short-term goals build the momentum and confidence needed to tackle bigger challenges.

Mars is our closest habitable neighbor and is approximately 140 million miles from Earth. Traveling to and living on the planet Mars presents a formidable long-term goal. However, Elon Musk, CEO of SpaceX, envisions a self-sustaining human colony on Mars to ensure the long-term survival of humanity. The gravity on Mars is 38% of that on Earth, allowing human beings to lift heavy objects. Musk's plan involves developing the Starship spacecraft to transport large numbers of people and cargo to the Red Planet. He has set ambitious timelines, aiming for uncrewed missions to Mars within the next few years, followed by crewed missions by the end of the decade. He emphasizes the importance of making life multiplanetary to guard against potential existential threats on Earth.[13]

SpaceX has experienced its share of setbacks, yet the company focuses on "fail-and-fix quickly" to move ahead. We may discount their willingness to make mistakes because Elon is a multi-billionaire, but tolerating mistakes is important. Mistakes cost time, energy and resources, but the cost of failure lessens if we follow basic principles.

First, we iterate quickly by identifying and resolving issues without investing excessive resources. This also means not being afraid to abandon a project. Deciding what *not to do* is as important as what *to do*. *Second*, we minimize risk through reusability, whether it be with templates, reusable technology, or prototypes. Taking inventory of current resources is key to making this happen. *Third*, we leverage technology using automation, affordable software, and scalable tools to reduce costs and enhance efficiency. We must do enough research to obtain tools that will *truly* save time and resources. *Fourth*, we start small before scaling to larger investments or projects. *Fifth,* we view failures as investments. Failure, if leveraged effectively, is our most valuable learning tool.

By starting small, we train our minds to focus on action rather than perfection. Tiny steps accumulate into big changes; with each success, our confidence grows. Setting and achieving goals become not just a practice but a way of life, propelling us toward a future filled with purpose and possibility. So, let us set our sights high. We start small—one step at a time—to watch our vision become reality.

CHAPTER FIVE

Creating a Purpose-Driven Life

*The "What ifs" can spark hope, inspiring
you to dream, to act and to believe
in possibilities yet to come.*

Sir Chris Hoy's journey to becoming one of the most successful Olympic cyclists in history with six gold medals was built on a foundation of small, deliberate steps aimed at continuous improvement. Rather than focusing solely on winning medals, Hoy concentrated on enhancing specific aspects of his performance, such as his start, acceleration, and technique. He set small, achievable goals throughout his training, measuring progress incrementally. This method allowed him to stay motivated and make measurable strides over time. By homing in on these tiny details, Hoy believed that the accumulation of marginal gains would ultimately lead to significant overall performance improvements.[14]

In addition to his physical training, Hoy also applied the concept of small steps to his mental preparation, working on short-term strategies to manage stress and pressure. He embraced the "marginal gains" philosophy, which emphasized making minor improvements across all areas, from his equipment to his mental resilience. This approach of consistently focusing on small, incremental progress ultimately led Hoy to become Britain's most decorated Olympic cyclist, proving that success is often the result of persistent, incremental efforts rather than one giant leap.

Regrets, Dreams and "What Ifs"

I can say with relative certainty that none of us want to live a life filled with regrets. We can easily find stories of entertainers who wish they had spent more time with their families. Others have focused mainly on a career and never had a family. Then, there are those who never pursued a lifelong dream because of fear or inaction. Questions often linger: *What didn't I do that I could have done? Why didn't I push harder to reach my potential? Did I truly maximize my skills and seize opportunities? Why didn't I seek the help I needed?*

What was I so afraid of? These reflections can haunt us, challenging us to mourn over what might have been.

It's natural to justify our past choices to soften the weight of regrets or rationalize the times we didn't act. This mental exercise helps to ease the guilt or disappointment that can creep into our thoughts, allowing us to move forward despite inaction or missteps. However, justifying the past doesn't change what happened, but it doesn't have to define the future.

Imagine a different outcome—one shaped by the courage and confidence of a life lived fully, right up to the end. Instead of retiring into aimlessness or shelving dreams indefinitely, what if we use our accumulated experience and freedom to pursue long-held aspirations? Life isn't about avoiding risks but embracing opportunities, even later in the journey, with the wisdom and resilience gained over time.

The "what ifs" of life don't have to be negative. They can spark hope, inspiring us to dream, to act and to believe in possibilities yet to come. The ability to keep dreaming—never to stop imagining what could be—is the key to a fulfilled life. It's about living with purpose, not regrets, and finding the strength to move forward, no matter our place on life's path.

Setting Age-Proof Goals

Most of us have seen the commercials with a cute green gecko that talks, so we've most likely heard of *GEICO*. At age 50, *Leo Goodwin Sr.* leveraged his background as an accountant and insurance agency manager to found GEICO alongside his wife, Lillian. Despite financial hurdles and skepticism from established insurers, Goodwin focused on serving a niche market—government employees and military personnel. This innovative approach helped GEICO grow into one of the largest insurance companies in the United States, illustrating how experience and persistence using a well-branded gecko can create lasting success.[15]

Our years of accumulated knowledge and skills set us apart in ways that younger generations can't replicate. Whether it's understanding industry nuances or anticipating challenges, our expertise allows us to navigate complexities with ease, or at least with a stamina that we've built over the years. Sometimes that stamina comes after picking ourselves off the floor after failures. Experience also builds credibility; people trust someone who has a proven track record. In a competitive landscape, this depth of understanding becomes our most valuable tool.

The Opportunity to Reinvent Yourself

Colonel Sanders (Harland David Sanders, 1890-1980) opened Sanders' Café, which was attached to a service station in Corbin, Kentucky. The Shell Oil Company had given him the service station in return for paying Shell Oil a percentage of his sales. Here, he served his fried chicken. In 1935, at age 45, he received the honorary commission as a "Kentucky Colonel" by the governor of Kentucky. By 50, he had finally perfected his "secret recipe" for his beloved fried chicken, prepared in a pressure cooker.

"Kentucky Fried Chicken" was coined by a sign painter named Rodney L. Anderson, and Sanders used the name to differentiate his product from the more common deep-fried southern chicken. In 1955 at age 65, he incorporated Kentucky Fried Chicken; by 1964, there were more than 600 franchises in the USA and Canada. He eventually sold KFC but continued to tour KFC restaurants around the world as the "face" of KFC.[16]

As we better understand our skills, true passions and priorities, the halftime years provide the perfect backdrop for reinvention and expansion. Whether it's starting a new career, launching a business, or pursuing a creative endeavor, midlife offers the clarity and freedom to align our efforts with what truly matters. Stories of reinvention provide proof and inspiration that it's never too late to grow and thrive. I can imagine that after he sold the company, with every visit Colonel Sanders made to a KFC around the world, he felt the impact of his legacy, a unique recipe and a solid business plan.

Defining Core Values and Living by Them

In today's rapidly changing business landscape, several companies have struggled to stay true to their core values while adapting to modern challenges. *Peloton's* new campaign launched on May 23, 2023, brought fitness offerings for all ages, levels, and walks of life. However, the company faced significant difficulties aligning its brand identity with shifting market demands.

Peloton, once synonymous with high-end fitness and exclusivity, saw a steep decline in revenue as the market evolved. Their marketing message was confusing. They had introduced a free membership tier and diversified their offerings to include Peloton Gym, attempting to cater to a broader audience. While these moves were aimed at revitalizing the brand, they also diluted Peloton's original value proposition of offering a premium, exclusive experience, leading to a potential identity crisis.[17]

Another example is *Nokia,* a company with a rich history in mobile technology. As Nokia transitioned from being a leading consumer brand to focusing on B2B technology, it struggled to maintain its traditional values of innovation and reliability while rebranding itself in a crowded market. The challenge was balancing the legacy of being a household name with the need to stay relevant in a new business arena, ultimately causing tension between maintaining their core values and embracing new strategies. Fortunately, by enhancing trust, recognition, and awareness, Nokia recovered by reconnecting with its main audience and expanding their customer engagement and impact.[18]

Staying Consistent with Your Values

Regardless of an organization's size or focus, defining core values is essential, as they are typically aligned with the brand's messaging. We are approaching core values and character in this book because the foundation of our character influences our responses when facing difficult or compromising situations. Professional core values that align with personal core values create a sense of authenticity and integrity, allowing individuals to navigate their work with confidence and consistency. This harmony between the personal and professional realms fosters a deeper commitment to one's work, leading to more meaningful and sustainable success.

As methods evolve and we implement new technologies, core values become even more critical. For it's easy to become distracted and misaligned from overarching goals. Alignment between our values and actions fosters trust—an important element to be developed and sustained with customers, shareholders, colleagues, and personal contacts. While methods and tools may change, core values provide the stability needed to weather uncertainty and change.

Defining Your Personal and Professional Truth

Regularly defining and reviewing core values creates a strong foundation for both personal and professional life. These values are crucial as they reflect your driving force and lay the groundwork for a clear purpose. Additionally, they cultivate a character of consistency and authenticity. When circumstances change, core values should be consistent and provide the stability to sustain us through difficult times or good times.

In defining our core values, we should think of some words to describe our lives, like honesty, follow-through, fairness, or a strong work ethic. These should be unmovable principles. When defining core values, we will center on two key areas—**faith and character**—while expanding on each. (More on core values appears in the *Appendix* of *Stop Circling* book[19])

In what or in whom we put our faith establishes our essential source of truth. Whether it's God, science, government, nature, or ourselves, this foundational core value creates a gravitational pull one cannot deny or escape. It is where we look to find wisdom in dealing with changing circumstances. Motivational author Zig Ziglar (1926-2012) once said, "The height of your success is determined by the depth of your belief."

While growing up, our family spent most of our vacations camping. Each summer, we visited different landmarks. I vividly remember entering the pitch-black darkness of the *Oregon Caves*. It was totally black until our guide struck a single match, instantly illuminating the entire cave. It was a powerful illustration of faith's role in our lives—faith acts as a guiding light, shaping our ultimate source of truth. Whether we place our trust in God, science, government, nature, or even yourself, this foundational belief creates a gravitational pull that shapes personal perspectives and decisions. It becomes the lens through which we seek wisdom to navigate life's changing circumstances.

Many rely on themselves for guidance because they do not trust leaders or feel disconnected from a seemingly silent God. In a world where every voice claims its own version of truth, confusion is an easy trap. The sentiment, "Everything is worthwhile except a strong opinion," can lead to endless indecision. Therefore, it's vital to evaluate the strength of our faith and the wisdom it provides. Once we've established this foundation, we can stop deliberating and act based on the convictions our beliefs inspire. Only through action can those convictions truly come to life.

My faith in a personal God has been a steady rudder, guiding me through many of life's challenges. I see His handiwork in nature and feel His profound presence in my daily experiences. I also recognize that many others are searching for that kind of connection. Interestingly, Bible sales increased by 22% in the first ten months of 2024, a trend confirmed by the *Wall Street Journal*.[20] I believe one reason for this surge is the growing search for solace, truth, and meaning in the face of rising anxiety and uncertainty.

Addressing Failures

Some believe it's essential to establish a ritual or evoke a specific feeling to gain favor or ease feelings of guilt. This strategy is evident in a scene from the 2016 movie *Burnt*, discussed in my book *Bad Code:*[21]

> In *Burnt*, chef Adam Jones (played by Bradley Cooper) epitomizes a life weighed down by regret. After his drug-fueled, obsessive pursuit of perfection destroyed his career and relationships, Adam imposed his own form of penance: shucking one million oysters at a bar in New Orleans. This act of voluntary self-punishment was his way of atoning for past mistakes. He meticulously tracked his progress in a small pocket notebook, secured with a rubber band, as if completing this task could somehow erase his guilt.

Penance, which means "to be sorry," serves a dual purpose: acknowledging wrongdoing and seeking to alleviate guilt. However, Adam's relentless act of oyster-shucking failed to address the deeper issues that caused his failures. Penance alone, while symbolic, didn't equip him to handle setbacks or rebuild his life. Many, like the character Adam, find themselves stuck in a cycle of self-reparation, hoping it will lead to a clean conscience and forgiveness. Yet what they truly need is a sense of purpose and a deeper source of renewal—something akin to a spiritual battery to jumpstart their lives.

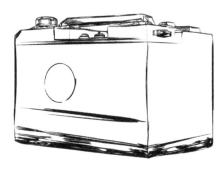

Belief in a higher power can be a transformative first step. Trusting in a supreme being provides the strength to confront feelings of guilt, shame, and failure while breaking free from the spiral of negative self-talk. This faith can anchor individuals with a light illuminating the darkness, helping them find meaning and direction amidst life's struggles. However, not everyone shares this belief, and many feel lost in their search for fulfillment. Without a sense of spiritual grounding, some individuals wander aimlessly, continually seeking some purpose or clarity that eludes them. The journey to healing often requires not just accountability but also a deeper connection to something greater than oneself.

The Role of Character and Integrity

The personal attributes of our character are what others see the most. We can structure these aspects of character into building blocks to form a strong, solid foundation. My character layers include respect, trust, dependability, thoroughness, initiative, and creativity, each with offshoots that apply to daily life.

Scheduling my days purposefully aligns with several key areas of personal growth, including thoroughness, initiative, and creativity. By prioritizing this practice, I'm not just organizing my time; I'm cultivating an attribute that integrates my core values. Over time, this focus shapes my approach to many aspects of life, reinforcing habits that promote balance, intentionality, and the ability to adapt creatively to challenges.

The question, "What do others see when they look at my life?" offers us considerations that not only apply to an outward appearance but also to inner qualities that create a lasting impact, such as character, convictions, and values that guide decisions and actions. These traits collectively shape the legacy we build and impact how others perceive our authenticity and integrity.

Guiding Contract for Your Life

My father came from the generation where a handshake with a verbal agreement became a contract. Many of those contracts were fulfilled out of respect stemming from a strong personal or professional relationship. In fact, after he passed, my sisters and I successfully followed up on some of those agreements that were still in place.

Handshake deals may still be found where personal relationships and trust play a key role in business but are not nearly as common. Many of today's contracts are filled with formal, precise, and legally binding language with clauses covering many vital aspects. It's important to carefully read these contracts.

How many of us have suddenly found ourselves in a precarious situation because we hadn't read the fine print of a contract? What seems like legalese on a credit card bill or employment contract suddenly stands out on the contract as a glaring reminder of ignored or missed details.

No matter what guiding force we choose for our lives, whether it's faith, circumstances, or self-preservation, We should examine it as a foundational principle upon which all other areas are built. Just like a building relies on strong piers and a solid foundation, our guiding force must be stable. Without a firm foundation, the structure is far more vulnerable to external influences and storms. The abiding truths that anchor my life have stood the test of time over centuries. This enduring wisdom and confidence provide clarity and stability, even in moments when understanding feels out of reach. It provides life's trusted "fine print."

CHAPTER SIX

Mastering the Mindset for Success

Neuroplasticity empowers individuals like you and I to view capabilities not as fixed entities but as dynamic and expandable potentials.

With grandchildren now in our lives, I'm reminded of the words, "No!" and "I can't!" It's a powerful reminder that, even as adults, our instinctive reaction to change is often, "I can't!" rather than embracing a growth mindset, "I can!" Hesitation and resistance are knee-jerk reactions, especially as we navigate the rapid advancements of technology and the changes they bring.

Our Brain is Wired for Learning and Change

The brain is a complex organ composed of various regions, each contributing to cognitive functions and behaviors that influence a growth mindset. Understanding the impact of different parts of the brain in fostering a growth mindset provides insights into the adaptability and flexibility in relation to our intelligence and skills.

Much discussion and many books explore the functions of the right and left brain, especially regarding creativity and how neuroplasticity affects different parts of the brain. Without delving into too much technical information, I will uncover some basic principles on the way our brain works and its influence on a *growth* mindset with clarity and resilience versus a *fixed* mindset of resistance.

In a **growth mindset**, individuals embrace challenges, persist in the face of setbacks, and see failures as opportunities for growth. In a **fixed mindset**, individuals avoid challenges for fear of failure and perceive effort as fruitless. Understanding this contrast is crucial for fostering resilience, adaptability, and a lifelong pursuit of learning. The brain weighs approximately three pounds and contains approximately eighty-six billion neurons—the most complex, powerful organ in the body.

When change looms on the horizon, it's natural to feel trepidation. While making a change often begins with a decision and the resolve of our will, equipping ourselves with deeper understanding provides insight and empowers us to face transitions more effectively. This information can inspire us to embrace life's pivotal moments with greater confidence, clarity, and even certainty.

The Science of Neuroplasticity Growth

Neuroscientific research consistently shows that the entire three pounds of the adult human brain is active and plays a role in various functions. At the heart of a growth mindset lies the remarkable phenomenon of *neuroplasticity,* an inherent quality of the brain that underscores its capacity to adapt and reorganize in response to experiences and challenges.

Neuroplasticity is a dynamic process that involves the formation of new neural connections and the reshaping of existing ones, allowing the brain to continuously evolve throughout an individual's life.[22] Let's imagine the first time we rode a bike. Most of us start by riding a tricycle or had training wheels for balance, but before long we were pedaling confidently on only two wheels. Years later, we still possess the basic skill, then enhance biking on a mountain bike or beach cruiser. This transformative ability highlights the potential for improvement and challenges the notion of fixed or unchangeable intelligence. This is encouraging information for any stage of life.

Ellen, a client of mine, is a midlife professional seeking a career change. Embracing a growth mindset, Ellen enrolled in a coding bootcamp despite having no prior experience in programming. Initially challenged by the complexity of coding languages, she persisted with her basic computer knowledge. As she actively pursued new information and honed her programming skills, *neuroplasticity* showed up. Her difficulties became opportunities for learning rather than insurmountable obstacles, for her brain adapted to the demands of coding, forging new neural connections. Ellen's *growth mindset*, coupled with the brain's plasticity, not only empowered her to become a proficient coder but also reshaped her perception of challenges. The outcome was increased confidence in applying her new skill to create the changes she desired.

As individuals engage in new experiences, acquire knowledge, and confront challenges, their brains undergo structural and functional changes. These alterations are a testament to the brain's adaptability, showcasing its responsiveness to the demands placed upon it. Neuroplasticity, therefore, serves as a beacon of hope. It empowers individuals like us to view capabilities not as fixed entities but as dynamic and expandable potentials.

The Role of the Prefrontal Cortex in Business Success

The *prefrontal cortex*, a dynamic and multifaceted region at the front of the brain, emerges as a central player in the realm of adopting a *growth mindset*. This critical area is closely associated with higher cognitive functions, including decision-making and goal-setting. As we engage in decision-making processes, the prefrontal cortex influences our approach to setbacks, influencing whether we perceive challenges as insurmountable obstacles or as opportunities for learning and improvement. Additionally, this brain region aligns with the belief that abilities can be developed through dedication and perseverance.

My friend Alex is a budding entrepreneur, who faced the challenges of launching a startup. He listened to podcasts and read about other startups to gain insight. Mostly, he learned how perseverance and wise counsel enabled others to overcome huge obstacles. When Alex struggled to gain visibility in a crowded market, he chose to refine his distinctiveness with a *growth mindset,* narrowing his market. He chose this setback not as a failure but as an opportunity to iterate and improve. Even though he didn't fully understand this at the time, Alex's prefrontal cortex guided strategic decision-making when the fear of failure reared its head, fostering resilience and adaptability.

Neuroscientific studies have illuminated the adaptability of the prefrontal cortex, showcasing its capacity to rewire and reshape in response to experiences and intentional efforts. Imagine the prefrontal cortex as electrical wires placed in various places for the easy and smooth flow of electricity through connections in the brain. The prefrontal cortex stands as an influential architect in constructing the mental framework for continuous learning, adaptability, and the pursuit of potential adopting a *growth mindset*.

How the Hippocampus Influences Decision Making

The *hippocampus* is nestled on each side of the inner brain, in areas shaped like seahorses, and plays a key role in a *growth mindset*. As it enables memory and learning, the hippocampus becomes particularly active when individuals actively seek out and engage with new information.

Mia was a student in midlife, who took on a challenging academic course. It wasn't easy to be around friends who didn't share her passion for learning. However, with a *growth mindset*, Mia actively strove to keep her mind sharp, embracing the idea that intelligence can be developed at any life stage. The hippocampus' memory and learning capacity played a crucial role in Mia's journey. When delving into complex subjects, the hippocampus facilitated the encoding and retrieval of information, allowing her not only to grasp challenging concepts but also to retain and apply them. Mia's confidence grew. So she was encouraged to pursue additional courses.

Picture the hippocampus as a bustling library in the brain. Each bookshelf represents a set of neurons, and each book is a piece of information or a memory. When we actively engage in learning or in new experiences, it's like pulling books off the shelves and flipping through the pages. Neurons spark to life, creating a dynamic dance as we absorb and process information. The more we learn, the more intricate and well-connected this library in our brains becomes. In the realm of a *growth mindset*, the hippocampus becomes a linchpin, reinforcing the belief that abilities and intelligence can be expanded through intentional efforts, no matter how old we are.

Prioritizing Health and Wellness

Even though this isn't a book primarily about health and wellness, maintaining good personal habits is key to overall well-being and a healthy mindset. I'm an early riser and like to get my workout in first thing while my husband prefers exercising later in the day. No matter when we exercise, staying active directly impacts energy levels, stamina, and sleep quality. We should not overlook the power of a simple walk—getting outside, especially in nature, is a great way to clear our minds and reset.

Nutrition also plays a huge role in energy and focus. Countless diets and programs are readily available, but it comes down to making smart choices. Eating a balanced diet supports brain function, mood, and overall health while lowering the risk of chronic disease. I love my afternoon handful of dark chocolate blueberries, justifying them for their antioxidants, but I know they'll eventually lead to an energy crash. To stay sharp for an intense project, I make a different dietary choice.

Sleep is another essential factor. When I was younger, I could push through with little rest, but now I see how much quality sleep impacts productivity, energy, mental clarity and well-being. Getting to bed early has been key for me. Everyone's schedule and body rhythm are different; it is a matter of finding what works. Research shows that chronic sleep deprivation increases the risk of heart disease, stroke, obesity, and dementia, which is reason enough to prioritize rest.[23]

Creating Your Ideal Lifestyle

Is it possible to create an ideal lifestyle? What elements are most important to consider when evaluating a life direction? If an individual has worked one position for many years, she may feel exhausted and desire a break. But after that break, what's next? Schedules related to work days, weekly responsibilities, and yearly commitments have to be evaluated. Some may imagine not working at all. If one had no restrictions financially, would that change her dreams or possibilities?

There are some who want or need to continue working in their same position as it provides stability, but if there's no reward for additional effort, starting a side project may be an option. This situation that I call "maintenance mode" creates a different window of opportunity.

One's personality, experience, and purpose are unique. Some of the biggest roadblocks in moving forward are fear, imposter syndrome, or feeling overwhelmed. It's easy to lose momentum if dreams are continuously postponed. When momentum is lost, confusion and indecision step in. When this happens, pursuing help and accountability will make a positive difference in moving forward.

Restarting or reinventing ourselves at midcareer or the halftime of life unlocks new opportunities by leveraging refined skills and experience with a growth mindset, as it's never too late to start. We are not too old, and today's technology can significantly boost our chances of success. Even as many low-level entry jobs fade, a commitment to lifelong learning and the rise of AI, will amplify our expertise and experience.

So it's time to dream again. Loving what we do and pursuing our ideal life—whether it's family time, caring for loved ones, travel, or launching a business—holds immense value. A strong foundation of core values ensures the years ahead are meaningful, impactful, and rewarding.

The basics will continue to be important. I am still somewhat surprised at the resurgence of vinyl records. Some of the analog recordings of the past will continue to hold value, even with digital technology at the forefront. In fact, some of those vinyl recordings hold more value today than when released. The songs are good, and the recording quality stands the test of time.

In the same way, the value of basic skills, experience and life principles will continue to hold importance, even with the rise of digital tools and AI. They provide a solid foundation for a future that's never certain, but with a growth mindset, full of possibility and fulfillment. So we should not let our dreams die, but also don't dismiss the strong foundation we possess for building that dream.

CHAPTER SEVEN

Application: Creating Your Ideal Lifestyle

Defining and achieving an ideal lifestyle requires intentional goal setting, a strong mindset, and clarity on personal values. This section will guide you through key application steps to design a fulfilling, sustainable way of life. If you take the time to reflect, revise, and apply these principles, your future self will thank you!

Assessment: HALFERS Tool™

The HALFERS tool™ helps evaluate seven key areas of life: **Health, Attitude, Learning, Finances, Employment, Relationships,** and **Spirituality**.

Take a moment to rate where you are with "A" for each area on a sliding scale from 0 to 100%. Then, reflect on where you'd ideally like to be with "B" for each one.

For a deeper dive into these categories, check out our book *Stop Circling*.[24]

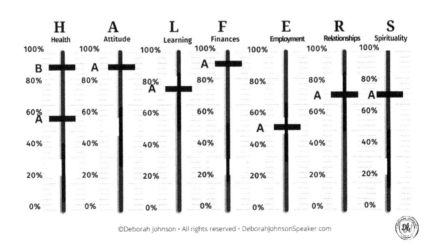

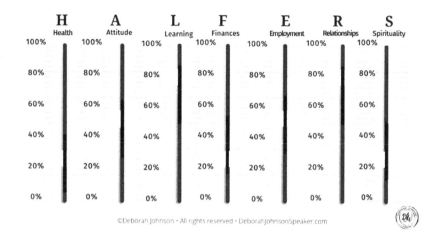

Goals: Define and Refine Your Vision

Setting meaningful goals is the foundation of creating an ideal lifestyle. Use the following steps to evaluate where you are and where you want to be. Refer to the individual evaluation using the HALFERS Tool™ to apply the following steps:

- Reflect on the past year: What was accomplished? What was missing?
- Write down any existing goals and assess whether they were achieved.
- Determine what goals need to be revised or eliminated—priorities may have shifted.
- Rephrase goals in a way that excites and motivates for the next steps.
- What goals should be set now to move toward an ideal life?

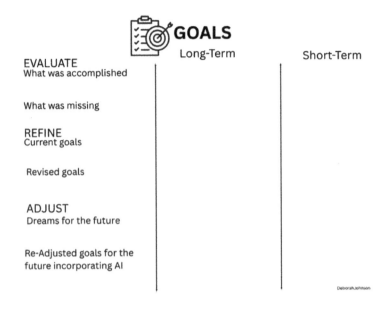

Mindset: Cultivate a Growth-Oriented Perspective

One's mindset is the driving force behind achieving personal goals. Engage in practices that strengthen mental adaptability and resilience. Define one application or goal for each of the areas below:

- **Applying Neuroplasticity**: Embrace new experiences, learn continuously, and challenge yourself. Even if you are not interested in coding, expanding your tech skills can open new opportunities.

- **Prefrontal Cortex Activation**: Set achievable goals with a structured system for follow-through. Utilize tools like accountability partners and goal-setting worksheets to accelerate progress.

- **Hippocampus Engagement**: Commit to lifelong learning. Sign up for online courses, coaching programs, or continuing education to expand your abilities.

- **Overcome Limiting Beliefs**: Avoid thoughts like "I'm too old" or "I'm not smart enough." Decide to create "new positive language" for those thoughts.

- **Mindset Shifts**: What perspectives or beliefs are needed to make individual dreams a reality?

Lifestyle: Design a Life That Aligns with Your Values

Now is the time to apply what you've learned and define what your ideal lifestyle looks like. Consider these practical key questions:

- **Work-Life Balance**: How many hours per week do you want to work? What kind of work would be most fulfilling?

- **Projects & Priorities**: What personal or professional projects have you postponed? How much time will you allocate to them?

- **Financial Needs & Aspirations**: What monthly income do you need to meet obligations? How much additional income would support travel and other goals?

- **Health & Well-being**: What habits, including nutrition and exercise, will help maintain a vibrant lifestyle?

- **Travel & Exploration**: What trips do you want to take over the next twenty years, including family visits and bucket-list adventures?

Final Thoughts: Your ideal lifestyle isn't just about setting goals but about aligning your daily habits, mindset, and long-term vision. Act today, adjust as needed, and enjoy the journey of creating a life that truly fulfills you. As you move into the next section of this book on creating a new way of doing business, keep the basics you've already built—both professionally and personally—front and center in your mind. They'll help ground you to explore new ideas.

PART THREE

Creating Your Ideal Business

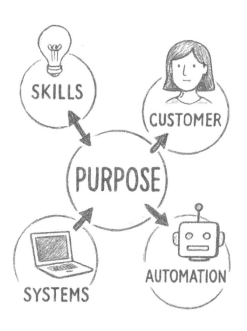

CHAPTER EIGHT

Building a Business with Purpose and Flexibility

*A well-defined mission serves as
a guiding star in business.*

Physical flexibility has never been my strength, even touching my toes takes effort. Yet, I've come to appreciate the benefits of balance, breath, and adaptability, incorporating yoga and Pilates into my routine with surprising results. The same principle applies to business. Flexibility, paired with a clear mission, is essential in navigating setbacks. Adjusting workflows or making tough personnel decisions is rarely comfortable, but staying anchored in a strong vision helps guide each step.

Just as a stargazing app reveals the vastness and clarity of the night sky, a well-defined mission serves as a guiding star in business. It brings focus to daily operations and strategic shifts, ensuring every decision aligns with long-term goals. In challenging times, this clarity provides stability, motivation, and direction, keeping us on course even when the journey is uncertain.

Commitment to Your Mission

A historical example of flexibility combined with a strong sense of purpose and mission can be seen in the life and leadership of *Mahatma Gandhi* (1968-1948) during India's struggle for independence. Gandhi's overarching mission was to achieve freedom for India from British rule, but over time, his methods evolved, demonstrating a remarkable level of flexibility while staying true to his core values of nonviolence and justice.

Initially, Gandhi focused on legalistic, moderate approaches, advocating for rights within the framework of the British Empire. However, as the situation evolved and the limitations of these methods became apparent, he shifted tactics, demonstrating flexibility. Gandhi introduced the strategy of nonviolent civil disobedience, starting with the Non-Cooperation Movement in the early 1920s and later the Salt March in 1930. Each of these movements was a calculated response to the changing political environment, yet they were always rooted in his commitment to nonviolence and the empowerment of ordinary Indians. Gandhi's ability to adapt his strategies while steadfastly adhering to his mission and values was instrumental in galvanizing the Indian population and ultimately achieving independence in 1947.[25]

Developing Mental Flexibility

Nelson Mandela (1918-2013) exemplified the power of flexibility combined with a strong sense of purpose. Despite being imprisoned for 27 years, he remained committed to dismantling apartheid, adapting his strategies as circumstances changed. Whether through peaceful negotiations or armed resistance, his unwavering mission led to the end of apartheid and his election as South Africa's first Black president in 1994.[26]

During our time in South Africa, we visited *Londolozi*,[27] a stunning 37,000-acre reserve adjacent to Kruger National Park. *(see photo)* The founders' deep-rooted family values shape every aspect of the experience, from personalized service to a strong commitment to conservation. Their philosophy reflects the belief that purpose and mission guide both individuals and organizations.

Mandela visited Londolozi multiple times, including on his long walk to freedom in 1991 after his release. His ability to evolve while staying true to his mission mirrors Londolozi's commitment to sustainability and community impact. As their website states, "Every night you spend at Londolozi you are responsible for the employment and welfare of five employees and their dependents. This doesn't include protecting the rhinos and education of children." By 2020, Londolozi and its partners had facilitated advanced digital learning opportunities for over 26,500 learners from neighboring children. Like Mandela, they understand that flexibility, guided by a clear mission, leads to lasting change.

With the growth and opportunity of using elements of AI and new technology, we can either feel overwhelmed or embrace aspects that will help us in our lives and businesses. However, it's crucial to anchor these changes in core values. Doing so ensures that innovations enhance, rather than undermine, our mission and vision. This balance allows us, whether personally or within a large or small organization, to remain agile and responsive. It also helps to maintain a strong, consistent identity that resonates with others that's authentic. Ultimately, while the methods may evolve, the principles that define our character must endure, providing stability and direction in an ever-changing world.

Overcoming Mental Barriers and Roadblocks

Mental barriers keep us from experiencing our best years and the most common barrier is *Imposter Syndrome*—a psychological pattern where individuals discount their accomplishments for fear of being exposed as a fraud, despite evident success. People experiencing this syndrome often attribute their achievements to luck rather than skill and feel unworthy of recognition, like a counterfeit. Common characteristics include perfectionism, overworking to prove competence, and an inability to internalize success. Even high achievers struggle with imposter syndrome, constantly fearing they don't truly deserve their position or accolades.[28]

For example, Tom Hanks, of *Big* (1988), *Forrest Gump* (1994), *Saving Private Ryan* (1998) and other film successes, has openly discussed his experiences with *imposter syndrome*. In an interview with NPR, he reflected on moments of self-doubt, stating, "No matter what we've done, there comes a point where you think, 'How did I get here? When are they going to discover that I am, in fact, *a fraud* and take everything away from me?'" Additionally, during an episode of the "Armchair Expert" podcast with Dax Shepard,[29] Hanks shared his feelings of *imposter syndrome* while working with director Paul Greengrass, expressing concerns about being "found out" despite his extensive career.

I have known many musical artists who, despite performing at high levels, struggle with self-doubt and insecurity. *Imposter syndrome* is a mental barrier that left unchecked can lead to chronic stress, burnout, and decreased self-confidence that hinders personal and professional growth. It can prevent individuals from seizing new opportunities, asking for promotions, or sharing their ideas, for fear they aren't "good enough." This mindset can also create a cycle of overcompensation—working excessively to prove one's worth—leading to exhaustion and diminished well-being. Recognizing and addressing imposter syndrome as a mental roadblock is crucial to overcoming self-doubt and embracing personal achievements.

Using Mental Hacks and Shortcuts

Shortcuts and mental hacks often promise an easier path but can lead to prioritizing quick gains over core values and long-term goals. Just as malware corrupts a computer, negative thoughts, unhealthy mindsets, and the habit of taking shortcuts can disrupt our thinking and keep us stuck in unproductive cycles. In my book *Bad Code*,[30] I compare these disruptive mental hacks to a computer hack—frustrating, disruptive, and capable of derailing progress. Identifying and removing this "bad code" is essential for overcoming mental barriers.

A major example of a hacking incident was the 2013 Target data breach,[31] where attackers used phishing emails to infiltrate a third-party vendor, leading to the theft of 40 million customers' financial data. Similarly, in 1986, the Space Shuttle *Challenger* disaster occurred due to a failure in the O-ring seals, a design flaw that was ignored despite engineers' warnings.[32] Both cases highlight the dangers of ignoring critical processes in pursuit of convenience or speed—whether in cybersecurity or high-stakes engineering.

Shortcuts in decision-making, like skipping critical safety checks or rushing through projects, often leads to costly mistakes, rework, and frustration. Phishing emails may look legitimate but lead to disaster—just as enticing opportunities that seem "too good to be true" often are. In business, cutting corners in ethics can result in legal trouble, financial losses, and reputational damage.

Whether in technology, business, or personal choices, bypassing essential steps usually creates more harm than the effort it was meant to save. In the long run, such shortcuts often waste time, energy, and resources, making the disciplined path the better choice.

CHAPTER NINE

Achieving Excellence in Your Work

Mental discipline is just as crucial as physical repetition in mastering any craft.

Achieving excellence in any field—whether athletics, the arts, or business—requires a mindset shift, focus, and commitment. Athletes refine their techniques and training to reach peak performance while musicians must adjust their practice methods to overcome challenges. A pivotal moment often comes when one realizes that their current approach isn't yielding results. For me, that moment arrived when my internationally known piano instructor made it clear that unless I changed my practice methods, I would need to find another teacher.

Commitment with Persistence and Patience

My tendency to move quickly led me to reinforce mistakes rather than correct them. After my instructor's warning, I learned to slow down, break the music into small sections, and practice deliberately. Over time, this disciplined approach became my new normal, leading to greater precision, improved performance, and ultimately, a successful career. The same principles—commitment, persistence, and patience—apply to achieving excellence in any area of life.

Jascha Heifetz (1901-1987) one of the greatest violinists of all time, exemplified this disciplined approach. He meticulously isolated difficult passages, practicing them slowly to perfect intonation and bowing. By focusing on detail and reinforcing accuracy through repetition, he built the muscle memory needed for flawless performances. His method highlights the power of intentional practice in mastering complex skills.[33]

Beyond physical practice, Heifetz also used mental rehearsal, visualizing the correct execution of difficult passages. (See the book *Heifetz As I Knew Him* by Ayke Agus[34] for more information.) Similarly, a piano instructor I worked with in college had worked nights on the railroad. He memorized music through visualization when he had limited practice time. His ability to achieve performance-level excellence despite time constraints reinforced the idea that mental discipline is just as crucial as physical repetition in mastering any craft.

Protecting Your Mindset

In a world filled with social media distractions and misleading messages, it's increasingly difficult to block out influences that seem harmless but ultimately pull us away from our purpose and values. Like malicious code draining a system's resources, these messages consume our time and energy, making them destructive.

Practicing "mental encryption" is like securing a device with a passcode—filtering out negative influences before they take hold. Just as encryption requires verification for access, we can train our minds to immediately counter distractions with focused, purposeful thoughts. This not only limits external noise but also helps regulate our inner dialogue, preventing self-sabotaging beliefs from taking root.

To combat negative self-talk, try reframing thoughts like "I can't do this" into "I can give this my best effort." Identifying energy drains—situations or people that leave us feeling depleted—can also help protect our mindsets. By developing intentional language and mental strategies, we create a safeguard against harmful influences, keeping our focus on what truly matters.

The Importance of Evaluation and Assessment

When we feel stuck or our strategies aren't delivering results, it's essential to step back, assess, and adjust our approaches rather than abandoning our missions. This process keeps our businesses aligned with their goals while reinforcing a resilient mindset that resists unhealthy external influences.

AI tools make data analysis easier, but the most valuable feedback often comes from customers and team members. When launching a new course or book, I've offered early access in exchange for reviews, providing direct insights. For larger businesses, market feedback is readily available through surveys, quizzes, or analytics. Sometimes, small adjustments can turn failure into success, but the real risk of failure lies in resisting change. Complacency, encapsulated in the attitude of "it's good enough now; we don't need to change a thing" is similar to neglecting watering or trimming a plant or tree because it looks good just as it is. Without a willingness to prune withering branches and to regularly water, little new growth or fruit will result.

A company that didn't fully embrace new growth was *Kodak*, founded in 1888 by George Eastman in Rochester, New York. Growing up, I was very excited to have my first Kodak Instamatic camera that was photo-ready simply by popping in a plastic film cartridge. I took picture after picture, sending in the exposed cartridges for development. Their slogan was, "You press the button, we do the rest."[35] Their innovation made photography accessible to the general public, eliminating the need for complex chemical processing. They also provided disposable cameras, very popular for weddings and celebrations.

Kodak engineer Steven Sasson developed the first digital camera in 1975. Despite this groundbreaking invention, Kodak was hesitant to embrace digital technology, fearing it would undermine its lucrative film business. Competitors like Sony and Canon adapted while Kodak clung to film believing it was "good enough." By the time they tried to pivot, the market had moved on, and Kodak filed for bankruptcy in 2012.[36] A willingness to change is more relevant and important than ever, particularly when it applies to AI. Doing business the way we've always done will leave us in a similar situation as Kodak.

Crafting a Mission Driven Business Model

If the market is giving negative feedback and we're feeling stuck or not seeing the positive results, it may be time to evaluate whether change or growth is needed. Are we relying on outdated methods because they feel comfortable? A successful, mission-driven life requires a mindset that is open to growth, continuous learning, and sometimes, the willingness to abandon old habits that no longer serve our goals.

We associate the phrase, "We've always done it this way" with an established company's old guard. There is nothing wrong with using tried and true methods, but with the explosive growth of AI and its ease of use, now is the time to consider using a wide range of tech tools. However, adopting new tools requires careful consideration; it's vital to maintain one's core objectives and values. Innovation demands a clear understanding of why these tools are being used—ensuring they serve a mission rooted in solid, well-considered values. Each unique story helps in defining one's individual mission.

The Power of Your Story

Stories have the power to connect us, providing a personal and relevant way to share experiences. Whether shaped by success, challenges, or failures, our unique stories influence how others see us and how we see ourselves. By openly sharing our journeys, we allow others to connect with our authentic selves, learn from our insights, and connect on a deeper level.

Failure is often where the most valuable lessons emerge, yet many leave these moments out, creating an illusion of unbroken success. The polished images we see online can be misleading, making it easy to believe that success comes without setbacks. But just like the "ugly duckling" before it becomes a swan, every story has its struggles. Ignoring these parts of our journey distorts reality and diminishes the power of perseverance. I find it inspiring to hear about the introverted girl from math class who becomes a news anchor or the former history classmate who sat in front of me who becomes the city's mayor. These stories highlight resilience, proving that setbacks and growth go hand in hand. The challenges we overcome shape who we become, making them essential elements of any compelling story.

Kat Hantas experienced this firsthand when her film about a boy band was abruptly derailed the day before release when the band broke up. Rather than letting the setback define her, she used her industry knowledge and connections to cofound *21 Seeds Tequila*. Her story, as told on *How I Built This with Guy Raz*,[37] is a testament to adaptability and persistence—proving that setbacks can be steppingstones to even greater success.

Discovering one's personal story takes intentional reflection, a deliberate process of analyzing experiences, actions, and outcomes to uncover the reasons behind success or failure. By embracing this practice, we open ourselves to continuous growth. I regularly evaluate my progress and identify areas for improvement. It takes time and effort, but even when it feels unnecessary, journaling and self-assessment help me validate my lifestyle and business. This practice is not just for business owners. Everyone experiences benefits by recognizing small achievements and appreciating the unique qualities that drive success. Success, based on personal values, brings even greater fulfillment.

Looking beyond skill and talent, I spend some time on self-evaluation. I know that persistence and consistency reside at the core of my drive. At first, these traits seemed ordinary, but I soon realized they are powerful differentiators, particularly in creative fields where follow through is a challenge. Recognizing these strengths helped me redefine success and appreciate the qualities that set me apart.

Passion vs. Expertise—Finding the Balance

Author Cal Newport uses Steve Martin's journey to success in his book *So Good They Can't Ignore You*,[38] as a powerful illustration of preparation over raw passion. Martin realized that to stand out in a saturated comedy market, he couldn't rely solely on a passion for comedy; instead, he dedicated years to honing a unique, meticulously crafted style. This approach required relentless preparation and focus on building a skill that would make his performances unforgettable. Martin's dedication to perfecting his craft—without shortcuts—ultimately led to his breakout success, embodying the principle that skill-building often surpasses raw passion in achieving lasting success.

THE POWER OF AFTER

Thomas Edison once remarked, "Opportunity is missed by most people because it is dressed in overalls and looks a lot like work."[39] When hard work and preparation meet opportunity, doors open that might have remained closed. Preparation isn't simply about acquiring skills; it's about consistently applying skills and experience to a goal, so that when opportunities do arise, the groundwork can maximize the effect. This blend of preparation and perseverance exemplify how success involves more than just initial excitement or passion; rather, it's a continuous investment in readiness and growth.

CHAPTER TEN

Building a Competitive Advantage

A clear and unique "Why" creates focus and resilience.

My husband was a pitcher with the Cleveland Indians. He had developed a solid pitching technique—throwing a nine-inch ball with precision and consistency. In the same way that a crowd's excitement builds when fastballs or curveballs strike out a hitter, audiences applaud musicians who execute flawless performances. Such expert performances are not random but the product of relentless practice and refinement where focus is on making each attempt as reliable as the last.

Developing these techniques requires continuous study and exploration, not only in practice but also in the commitment to learning and refining a craft. Hal David, part of the iconic songwriting duo Bacharach and David,[40] once shared that he read extensively—2,000 words for each lyric he wrote. This depth of study fosters a broadened perspective and allows for amplified imagination, creativity, and intuitive growth. As we dive deeper into learning, our insights evolve, allowing us to bring both precision and originality into our work, whether in the arts, sports, or other fields where mastery is the goal.

Defining Your Unique "Why"

A clear and personal "why" provides direction and purpose, fueling perseverance through challenges. More than just motivation, it creates focus and resilience. While it may not make us leap out of bed every morning, it sparks enthusiasm, making daily efforts feel meaningful and fulfilling. This inner drive, rooted in our uniqueness, is often the difference between simply working and truly thriving.

Kat Hantas' journey with *21 Seeds Tequila*[41] illustrates the power of staying true to a unique vision. The founders found success by trusting their instincts—crafting flavors and branding that resonated authentically with their audience. However, when they veered away from this intuition, they wasted time and resources. Their experience underscores the importance of a strong, distinctive purpose in guiding decisions and shaping an effective marketing strategy. This is a good reminder for any entrepreneur when tempted to follow market trends.

Developing a Competency Bank

A young mom recently voiced her concern about re-entering the workforce since her days were spent holding her six-month-old daughter and chasing her energetic two-year-old son. She had left her legal career to care for her children—a decision she didn't regret but one that left her wondering about her future. Whether stepping away from a job entirely or balancing part-time work with family responsibilities, raising a family is a period of immense change and adjustment.

My mother once gave me the book *Total Beauty and Fitness Programme*[42] by the glamorous *Raquel Welch* (1940-2023). Welch noted that one of life's busiest times is becoming a parent. A new baby brings sleepless nights, exhaustion, and the overwhelming responsibility of caring for a tiny life. Soon, simple routines like bedtime and shopping evolve into managing dance programs, music lessons, and sports. Many parents also juggle work, stretching schedules and stress levels to the limit. At times, it can feel like a mother's brain is as mushy as the oatmeal her child flings across the room.

In our conversation, I noticed a lack of confidence expressed in our friends' words—something many experience but rarely acknowledge. The skills gained from raising a family are often undervalued, yet they are significant. Time management, multitasking, conflict resolution, and problem-solving are all sharpened through parenting. I assured her that these competencies, when recognized and articulated, are assets in any workplace. Whether staying home full-time or balancing work and family, the experience builds a powerful "competency bank" of skills that can be leveraged when re-entering the workforce.

These are some of the skills that are developed when raising a family:

- Time Management, Prioritization and Organization
- Communication, Conflict Resolution and Negotiation
- Problem-Solving, Decision Making and Persuasion
- Teamwork, Collaboration, Leadership and Emotional Intelligence
- Creativity, Resourcefulness, Financial Management and Intuitiveness

Hard vs. Soft Skills—What Matters Most?

Soft skills are just as essential as hard skills and are a key part of any skill set. These include relational management and human resource abilities developed throughout a career. A hard skill that is highly valuable is research, especially in an AI-driven world. Professionals who can analyze data, synthesize information, and present coherent insights are in high demand. For instance, the medical insurance industry needs experts to interpret policies and communicate options to corporations. Mastering research tools—especially in combination with AI—can create significant opportunities in today's evolving workforce. This work can be done remotely as well.

Hard Skills

A specific ability or knowledge that is learned and teachable that's measurable and often gained through training or education.

Soft Skills

A personal attribute or trait that influences how effectively you interact, communicate and work with others.

examples:

Hard Skills	Soft Skills
Data Analysis	Communication
Project Management	Adaptability
Coding/Programming	Leadership
Foreign Language Proficiency	Emotional Intelligence
Financial Forecasting	Problem-Solving
Graphic Design	Time Management
Search Engine Optimization (SEO)	Collaboration
CRM Software Proficiency	Critical Thinking

application: Customer Service, Human Resources and Sales!

Deborah Johnson

In a data-driven, technology-focused market, soft skills are more valuable than ever. According to LinkedIn, the top five soft skills in demand in 2020 were *creativity, persuasion, collaboration, adaptability, and emotional intelligence.*[43] Many people already possess these skills, whether through corporate experience or balancing work and family life; they just need to own them. When struggling with a tech issue on my stationary bike, I appreciated the woman on the phone line who not only listened but also called with a creative solution. This is one of the reasons I stayed with the fitness company.

While hard skills like sales, computing, and production can be taught, soft skills develop over years of experience, often unconsciously. Forbes ranked complex problem-solving as the most desirable skill for success, followed closely by critical thinking.[44] Any parent knows firsthand the challenges of both. Studies suggest that over 70% of workplace challenges stem not from competition or logistics but from people and personalities. As employees return to offices, the demand for strong soft skills will only increase. Unlike hard skills, relational abilities cannot be learned in a classroom or purchased as a product, yet they hold immense value in today's job market. Effective communication, conflict resolution, and interpersonal skills are crucial in business, especially within family-owned enterprises.

Many family businesses fail due to personality clashes or the lack of a succession plan. *Anheuser-Busch*, a five-generation brewing empire, was sold to *InBev* in 2008 after internal disagreements weakened the company's position.[45] This illustrates how investing in skilled mediators with strong relational abilities could prevent costly disruptions. While legal counsel is essential, without effective communication, no workable plan can move forward. For example, *The LEGO Group* faced similar internal conflicts but successfully implemented structured family meetings, board discussions, newsletters, and an internal communication platform. These initiatives fostered transparency and trust among family members and executives to resolve disputes and align company goals.[46]

Understanding the Market Demand

We often find surprising inventions that eventually become essential in our lives. From toothpaste, promising a brighter smile to shampoo, claiming to make hair thicker, many products promise a must-have ingredient for beauty and youth. While some claims seem outrageous—like an electric face mask from the '90s or smooth sand from the 2000s—they often rely on clever marketing rather than actual innovation.[47]

Successful infomercials aren't just lucky—they're the result of extensive research and strategic planning. Companies invest heavily in market analysis, studying competitors and identifying gaps before launching a product. They don't just replicate what's already available; they add a unique twist, like a special feature, ingredient, or benefit. That uniqueness becomes their selling point, making their product stand out in a crowded marketplace.

We can use *Febreze* as an example. Initially launched as an odor-neutralizing spray, it flopped despite a $100 million marketing campaign. P&G responded by adding a fresh scent and repositioning it as a way to make homes smell clean and inviting. The commercial's imagery—green smoke vanishing with a few sprays—shifted consumer perception, turning Febreze into a household staple. The key to its success was not just functionality but the emotional connection it created with cleanliness and freshness.[48]

While we may not have massive advertising budgets, we can research our field and identify what makes our products or services unique. Copying others may lead to commoditization and price wars; a race to the bottom on pricing isn't sustainable. Instead, success comes from offering a fresh perspective or an improved version of an existing idea that resonates emotionally with the customer.

Consider Elton John, who once credited Bach, Beethoven, and Mozart for influencing his music.[49] Their timeless melodies shaped his songwriting, demonstrating how innovation stems from a strong foundation. In fact, the Bach chorales would have held much more interest if I could have associated them with the music of Elton John while analyzing them in my music theory courses. Similarly, by analyzing the market, finding our own angle, and crafting a unique value proposition that solves a problem, we create offerings that command attention.

CHAPTER ELEVEN

Positioning Yourself in the Marketplace

Discovering your core passion not only explains past career choices but also shapes future directions.

As a middle schooler with two younger sisters, I loved creating "schoolwork" for them. I used a typewriter with carbon paper to make fill-in-the-blank lessons. Looking back, I realize that content creation—whether for school, music, or other projects—has always been my passion. While many might assume this would lead me to a teaching career, I took a different path as an entrepreneur and performer. Yet that same creative spark continues to drive my work in creating albums, musicals, courses, and books.

Exploring the Heart of Your Purpose

Discovering our core passion not only explains past career choices but also shapes future directions. The concept of a "Core Common Denominator®" involves identifying a recurring theme or characteristic that connects our passions over time. To start, we reflect on what we've consistently loved—whether in childhood, college, or later in life. While each stage may seem distinct, a common thread often emerges, revealing what truly motivates us.

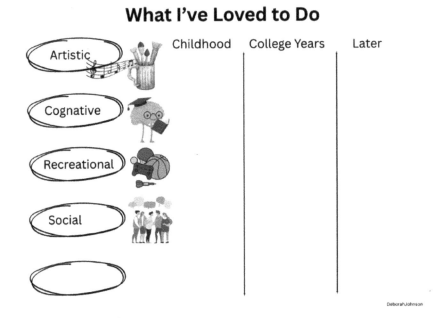

Consider *Alina Morse*, who, at just seven years old, envisioned a tooth-friendly lollipop. With determination and family support, she launched *Zolli Candy*, a sugar-free treat company that, by 2018, was in 25,000 stores and generating $6 million in sales.[50] Similarly,

Justis Pitt-Goodson discovered his passion for fashion at 13, using a sewing machine gifted to him by a teacher to create clothing. He later co-founded *BrownMill Clothing*, a thriving bespoke streetwear brand earning over £256,000 annually, even attracting NBA players.[51]

These stories highlight how early passions, when pursued with dedication, can evolve into successful ventures. Identifying and nurturing the steps in the Core Common Denominator® can provide clarity in both personal and professional growth, ensuring one's work remains aligned with what an individual truly loves.

Identifying Your Most Valuable Skills

Once you've identified what you love to do, the next step is recognizing what you're good at—skills or talents that may overlap with passions or stand apart. Reflect on different stages of your life, from childhood to adulthood; then, pinpoint activities where you've consistently excelled. These abilities often hold the key to shaping your personal and professional direction.

Maybe you feel irrelevant, uncertain of your worth, or hesitant to re-enter a fast-paced, tech-driven market. How do you assess your skills? Are you undervaluing them? Your experience and abilities could be more valuable than you realize if you take the time to evaluate them properly.

Recognizing the market value of your strengths at halftime can be life-changing. When you understand your worth, your mindset shifts, allowing you to envision a fulfilling, viable future. This awareness opens new possibilities, so you can strategically position yourself for fresh opportunities.

Many who launch entrepreneurial ventures realize their most valuable skills stem from years of experience, specialized knowledge, and wisdom. AI will likely replace entry-level tasks such as note-taking, spreadsheets, emails, and first drafts of content. However, those who understand how to use AI effectively can turn it into an advantage, creating new opportunities rather than losing ground.

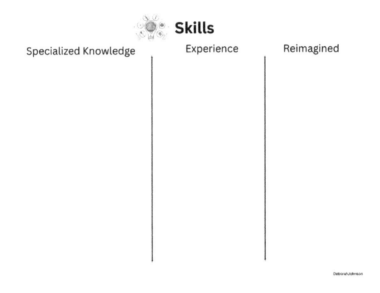

Studies show that women often rate themselves as less confident than men until their mid-40s, after which their confidence growth outpaces men by more than three times.[52] This explains why many hesitate to apply for jobs or take risks unless they meet nearly all qualifications. But confidence is built on an accurate assessment of skills and experiences, including those gained through failure. Self-reflection and focus are crucial. Just as clearing clutter helps sharpen focus, organizing your skills and strengths clears the way for greater productivity and success.

A great example of aligning skills with passion is *Palmer Luckey*, a technology enthusiast who developed an early love for gaming and engineering. His deep interest in electronics led him to create VR headsets and military-focused technology, industries that reflect both his love for innovation and strategy. Luckey's defense technology company, *Anduril Industries*, has developed surveillance systems utilized by U.S. Customs and Border Protection (CBP) along the southern border. These systems include autonomous surveillance towers equipped with sensors and artificial intelligence to detect and track movement. While the primary focus has been on fixed installations, *Anduril* has also integrated drone technology into its surveillance solutions.[53] Though he doesn't consider himself a celebrity, his inventive genius has made a significant impact. His story demonstrates how combining passion with skill can lead to groundbreaking achievements.[54]

Take time to journal and explore what you love and where you excel; these connections form your competency bank, a unique combination of skills that fuel growth and opportunity. Cal Newport refers to this as "career capital" in *So Good They Can't Ignore You*[55]—the expertise that sets you apart. This process is not just insightful but also enjoyable, offering clarity on your strengths and guiding you toward a fulfilling, purpose-driven life. Use your worksheet to track these insights to uncover valuable patterns.

The Pyramid of Value—Where do You Stand?

Maslow's pyramid of value outlines five levels of human motivation, starting with basic physiological needs and progressing toward self-actualization.[56] A 2025 article expanded on these needs, applying them to career choices.[57] Early in our careers, we often prioritize jobs that provide financial stability, healthcare, and security—sometimes at the expense of passion or long-term goals. As we gain stability, we seek roles that foster meaningful relationships, leadership opportunities, education, and creativity, allowing for greater impact and purpose.

By mid-career or halftime in life, there's often more freedom to pursue personal passions, creativity, and legacy-building work. These roles align with deeper missions and artistic expression, offering fulfillment beyond financial necessity. As our skills and experience grow, we naturally move higher on the pyramid, giving us more career choices that align with our values and aspirations.

Crafting a Compelling Selling Proposition

A selling proposition clearly defines the unique value a product, service, or business offers, setting it apart from competitors. It answers the essential question: *Why should a customer choose this over other options?* A strong selling proposition first solves a problem, then highlights what makes the brand memorable—whether through superior quality, affordability, exceptional service, or innovation. By effectively communicating this value, businesses can attract their ideal audience and build customer loyalty.

As an example, with over 4,933 cosmetic and beauty product businesses in the U.S. as of 2024, competition in the market is fierce.[58] Simply offering organic or ethically sourced products is no longer enough to stand out since those features have become industry standards. To break through, brands must craft a compelling, distinct message that resonates with consumers. While your angle may evolve, most innovations build upon existing ideas rather than reinventing the wheel. Unless you're creating the next theory of relativity or a groundbreaking invention, success often comes from refining and differentiating what's already in the marketplace. Thorough research is essential in identifying a unique angle that captures attention and adds real value.

Timeless marketing principles, like customer validation, still hold power. For instance, a crowded restaurant parking lot signals better food compared to an empty competitor across the street. Likewise, a friend's enthusiastic recommendation carries more weight than a traditional advertisement. Social proof and strong positioning remain key elements in making a selling proposition effective.

CHAPTER TWELVE

Crafting Simple and Clear Messaging

History shows that businesses able to adapt tend to succeed in tough times.

When crafting a selling proposition, start by writing down all your ideas. While you may feel clear about your offer, the goal is to define it in a way anyone can understand. Donald Miller, author of *StoryBrand*,[59] calls this the "grunt test," which evaluates whether a website's message is so clear that even a caveman could understand it in five seconds. It must answer three questions: What do you offer? How will it make my life better? How can I buy it? It's essential to be specific about what you're selling, who will use it, and where it will be used.

How to Search for Opportunities

Research plays a crucial role in refining your proposition. Many free and paid tools are available to help gather insights. Start by identifying searchable and relevant keywords. For example, Google Ads (a free tool) might show that "face cream" receives between 10K-100K monthly searches but with high competition. Ideally, you'll target keywords with lower competition to improve visibility. Tools like the *REFINE KEYWORDS* feature can help explore variations, including brands, skin types, and ingredients. YouTube, owned by Google, is another valuable resource for discovering top-ranking search terms in your niche.

For organic (free) research, try Google.com and analyze the number of results for your search term. You can refine your searches using Boolean operators like AND, OR, and NOT for precision. The plus (+) sign ensures a word must appear in results, while enclosing a phrase in quotation marks (" ") finds exact matches. AI tools can also assist in keyword research, but always review and edit the results carefully to ensure accuracy. Other tools like Ubersuggest, Ahrefs, and SEMrush are also available; however, they generally follow the same search principles.

Beyond digital tools, consider surveying potential customers to understand what they're searching for. Keep surveys concise and easy to complete. Research is an ongoing process, and while automated options exist, there's no substitute for actively uncovering your unique selling proposition. Keeping organized notes will help refine your messaging and strategy over time.

The Power of Repurposing and Diversification

Once you've clearly defined your *selling proposition*—what makes it unique and how it stands out from competitors—it's time to explore ways to repurpose or diversify your offering. This concept, often called "double-dipping" or even "triple-dipping," allows you to maximize value using your own content. Even if you don't implement every idea immediately, brainstorming now will provide a roadmap for future growth. Start with your main offering at the center and branch out with different ways it can be adapted or expanded.

For example, a music album isn't just a collection of songs; it can be sold as individual MP3s, performed live, turned into sheet music, or repurposed as an online course. Similarly, during the global shutdown, restaurants that pivoted to offer curbside pickup and delivery not only survived but often thrived. Some even introduced new menu options and service models that became long-term revenue streams. A crisis can drive innovation, and expanded services often remain viable beyond the initial challenge.

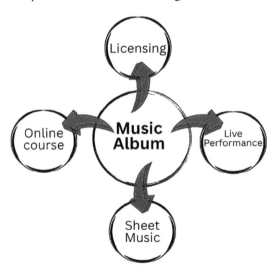

History shows that businesses that adapt succeed in tough times. During the 2008 Great Recession, discount retailers like *Dollar Tree* thrived by meeting consumer demand for budget-friendly essentials.[60] Their ability to provide low-cost necessities resonated with cost-conscious shoppers, proving that diversification isn't just about expansion but about staying relevant when conditions change. For service-based industries, engaging clients through online courses, webinars, or digital content can maintain an active client funnel. If you have intellectual property, consider repurposing materials into free resources that lead to paid offerings—a strategy widely used across industries. Your ultimate goal is to solve customer problems in multiple ways. Don't let fear of technology hold you back; many user-friendly tools exist to help repurpose content, build order forms, and streamline processes. Start with your core offering, explore creative ways to expand, and build a sustainable, scalable business.

Identifying Your Ideal Customer

You may already have a general idea of your ideal customer, but now is the time to refine it, especially if making changes in your focus. Understanding their *worldview* is crucial, as it influences their purchasing decisions and preferences for products or training. Consider where they spend their time, what they read, which conferences they attend, and how they make purchases—these insights will help you craft a targeted approach.

Conferences, both in-person and virtual, offer valuable opportunities to connect with potential customers. Over the years, I've booked clients and events through regional conferences and continue to gain meaningful connections at select gatherings. The rise of hybrid events has expanded reach, allowing businesses to engage with a broader audience while maintaining local relationships. This shift creates new opportunities for networking and customer acquisition on a global scale.

Building lasting connections should always be a priority. While researching and identifying your ideal customer is essential, it's an ongoing process that evolves as you engage with groups, organizations, and events. Staying connected through newsletters, podcasts, emails, and messaging platforms helps maintain relationships. Referrals have been a major source of opportunities in my work, serving as a reminder that consistent engagement is key to keeping connections fresh and valuable.

Historically, sellers have found creative ways to attract customers, such as street vendors in 19th-century London who sang, "Won't You Buy My Sweet Blooming Lavender" to sell their goods. The phrase "sixteen branches for a penny" refers to the affordable price of their goods.[61] I performed this song in high school, walking around a room full of tables, tossing bits of lavender to the audience. While modern marketing has evolved beyond street cries, the fundamental principle remains the same—capturing attention and making products memorable. Today, businesses still use product sampling at street fairs, proving that timeless methods of engagement continue to be effective.

When positioning your product, consider both the customer's needs and the product's unique benefits. For example, marketing lavender oil today would likely emphasize purity and quality to command a higher price and differentiate it from lower-cost alternatives. Without clear differentiation, products risk becoming

commodities. Reviews and recommendations help build credibility, but compelling, clear and simple messaging is equally vital in communicating what sets a product apart. AI tools can assist with refining descriptions, but remember, a well-crafted prompt ensures the best results. Clarity is key!

Why a Good CRM Matters

A solid Customer Relationship Management (CRM) system keeps all your interactions with current and potential customers organized in one place. A good CRM can send you reminders, automate emails, streamline your sales and marketing efforts, and offer insights to guide smart business decisions.

For teams, it also keeps everyone on the same page with up-to-date customer info. Some CRMs even offer detailed analytics and reporting tools, which can boost efficiency, improve customer retention, and ultimately increase profits. My advice? Choose one that's easy to use. *HubSpot* has a free version that works great for most entrepreneurial businesses.

CHAPTER THIRTEEN

Buying Freedom through Smart Financial Decisions

Understanding the distinction between appreciating and depreciating assets helps guide smarter financial and creative decisions.

When, free from debt, you can experience true financial and career freedom, especially at mid-career or halftime. This is especially relevant when building a lifestyle and business you love. As of Q4 of 2024, the average household credit card debt reached approximately $11,303,[62] with interest rates exceeding 20%—the highest in over two decades.[63] These rising costs, combined with inflation and a culture of spending on larger homes, cars, and convenience purchases, make debt accumulation easier than ever.

Keeping an Eye on the Money

Entrepreneurs and businesses of all sizes must carefully manage cash flow. Many successful startups have faced setbacks due to a lack of funds for growth or survival. As a creator, I prioritize financial vigilance—to sustain my work and to invest in marketing and development. Personally, I avoid carrying credit card balances to prevent interest charges; I make it a priority to pay off my card each month, which isn't always easy.

A default budget for both personal and business expenses is essential. In chapter 27 of my book, *Stuck is Not a Four-Letter Word*,[64] I discuss the importance of defining basic living costs—housing, food, medical, insurance, and debt in a default budget. Tracking monthly and annual expenses provides clarity and control, empowering better financial decisions. Understanding exactly where your money goes is the first step toward financial security.

 Default Budget

Includes:
- Living Expenses-monthly house, water, gas, electric
- Car Expenses-lease, monthly payment, maintainence, insurance
- Personal Expenses-grooming products, hair, clothing
- Food-groceries, eating out
- Medical Expenses-doctor, dentist, medication
- Insurance-life, casualty, additional house
- Debt-credit card, additional loans
- Business Expenses-marketing, equipment, payroll, domain, hosting
- Educational Expenses-conferences, continuing education
- Entertainment-movies, travel
- Phone & Internet-including cable, TV
- Extra-computer, furniture
- Savings

DeborahJohnson

One of the best ways to combat inflation is to evaluate spending habits with a clear budget. My husband has maintained a yearly budget for our family for years, and reviewing our expenses is always eye-opening. While certain costs are necessary, extras like food delivery and specialty coffee quickly add up. Budgeting doesn't mean eliminating all luxuries but being aware of spending and making intentional choices. Free tools like *Nerdwallet* help distinguish essentials from extras, making financial planning easier.[65] Most importantly, avoid unnecessary credit card debt, as delayed expenses come with steep interest. Paying your balance each month is a strong habit to maintain, but if you carry debt, focus on reducing it as quickly as possible. While I don't believe in cutting up credit cards entirely—since they can be useful for emergencies—using them wisely is key to long-term financial freedom.

Understanding Appreciating vs. Depreciating Assets

Most cars are depreciating assets, losing value over time unless they are rare classics. A friend once bought a *Peugeot*, calling it an "investment"; however, the car spent more time in the shop than on the road. Similarly, my husband and I purchased a used *Volvo* station wagon, believing it to be a smart choice. Despite the salesman's assurances of its safety and reliability for our young family, the engine started smoking as soon as we left the lot. Instead of returning it immediately, we held on, racking up repair bills before finally struggling to give it away.

In contrast, appreciating assets tend to increase in value, with a home being the most common example. Intellectual property, such as books, music, or characters, can also appreciate, though their true value is often uncertain during creation. Iconic figures like Disney's *Mickey Mouse* have generated billions, but the path to such success is unpredictable. While creative projects can be valuable, their financial return isn't always immediate or guaranteed. For creators, the drive to keep producing is strong, but not everything will yield long-term financial gains. Many books or music pieces generate modest direct revenue yet open doors to other opportunities. Understanding the distinction between appreciating and depreciating assets helps guide smarter financial and creative decisions.

Conducting Quarterly Business Reviews

I may not come from a sports background, but I know that in football, winning individual quarters increases the chances of winning the game. The same applies to basketball, even with its two halves instead of four quarters. In business, this concept translates to breaking the year into manageable segments to track progress and adjust strategies accordingly to create a win for the year.

A team doesn't have to dominate every quarter to succeed in sports or business. Winning just two quarters out of four can still secure a victory. In business, recognizing trends throughout the year allows for better planning of promotions, budgets, and ongoing projects. By analyzing performance in smaller increments, one can make proactive adjustments rather than waiting until year-end.

For years, I skipped quarterly reviews, only tallying expenses and income at tax time. However, I've since realized the immense value of regular check-ins, even as a small business. Reviewing results every quarter gives me clarity on what's working, what needs improvement, and what should be eliminated. It's a simple yet powerful habit that can significantly impact long-term success.

CHAPTER FOURTEEN

Application: Creating Your Ideal Business

These insights are highly practical and will help you align your purpose with your unique strengths. Let's make sure you're not just dreaming but actively working toward creating the business with a lifestyle that fits who you are.

To Set Yourself Apart: Four Principles to Apply

One: Define a Unique Strength Based on Your Story

Identify a strength that sets you apart—something tied to your personal experience or background. This becomes your differentiator in the marketplace.

What's a strength you have that others either haven't tapped into yet—or aren't good at? That strength could be the foundation of a new business opportunity. If you can figure out how to turn it into income, you're well on your way to building a stand-alone business. Don't forget—being different is what makes you stand out.

Here's a simple exercise: do a quick online search to see what's already out there in your space. For example, when I searched "leadership speakers," Google gave me 255 million results! If I simply called myself a "leadership speaker," how would I ever rise above the noise? The answer? Get specific. Draw from your own personal story. That's where the value and uniqueness live, and honestly, it can be fun, too. One of my main focuses is self-leadership for creatives, or for those who imagine themselves as creative. Because of my unique background in production and performance, I'm able to put a fresh, colorful spin on core principles like mindset, habits, systems, and goals.

Take a little time to reflect and journal. What experiences have helped shape you? What unique qualities do you bring to the table? Whether you're an entrepreneur, a small business owner, or even a volunteer, your background matters. It just might be your secret edge.

Two: Put Your Transferable Skills into a Repeatable System

Take the skills you've gained and organize them into a system that you can build a business around—something sustainable and aligned with your goals and lifestyle.

As you work through the "Core Common Denominator" chart, take time to assess both your hard and soft skills. Then brainstorm ways those skills can be applied in areas that not only match your passions but also support the lifestyle you're aiming for. If you're not quite at the point of financial freedom, part of your system should include a realistic plan to get there.

Include both long and short-term goals in your overall strategy. Review them at least once a quarter and adjust as needed—keeping a lifelong learning mindset. When setbacks come (and they will), track them and look for the lessons. If you're learning and growing from the experience, it's not really a failure but a steppingstone to resilience. Don't forget to revisit your purpose and mission regularly. It's a great way to validate what makes you unique. Your "why" is what fuels your motivation. Staying connected to it will help keep you focused and moving forward.

Three: Commit to Lifelong Learning and Use Automation

> *Stay open to continual growth, and don't shy away from technology. Automation can help streamline your business, save time, and boost efficiency.*

Keep reminding yourself that learning and growing—both personally and professionally—are ongoing parts of your journey. With so much e-learning content available every single day, there's no shortage of ways to get support or training. Staying in learning mode is a key part of thriving in today's world.

Also, keep an open mind about how you might automate more parts of your business. We'll dig deeper into that in Part Four of this book. Just know this: automation isn't just for big corporations. It's a powerful tool that can simplify and streamline your business *and* your life. Don't let technology intimidate you. Learn enough so you can confidently find the right people to help where needed.

Four: Measure and Adjust for ROI (Return on Investment)

Track what's working and what's not. Be willing to adjust your strategy based on results, and always recognize the value of your time, effort, and progress.

Figuring out your return on investment—especially when you're starting something new—can feel tricky. Yes, it often takes some money to make money, but that doesn't mean you need a huge investment up front. Don't get overwhelmed by the numbers. Give yourself grace and the time it takes to build momentum.

Pay attention to your results. What's working? What's not? If something isn't giving you the outcome you hoped for, tweak your approach and try again. Keep experimenting until you find your rhythm. When you need a little inspiration, check out business stories like those on the *How I Built This* podcast. They're great reminders that every success story had a starting point. Finally, celebrate your strengths. You have unique wins and qualities worth recognizing. Take time to appreciate what sets you apart.

Quick Tips for Financial Health

- **Avoid investments that lose value over time.** Think twice before putting money into things that depreciate quickly—like certain cars, gadgets, or trendy items.
- **Set aside funds for extras.** Open a separate account for things like vacations, holidays, or special treats so those expenses don't throw off your regular spending plan.

- **Pay off credit card debt as quickly as you can.** High-interest debt drains your finances. Tackle it with urgency.
- **Create a realistic, workable budget** that fits your lifestyle and financial goals. Review it at least quarterly—or twice a year at a minimum—and make adjustments as needed. If you don't have a default budget, create one.
- **Be honest with yourself about your spending.** Facing the truth about where your money is going is the first big step toward real change.
- **Remember that inflation comes in cycles.** It won't last forever. If you need perspective, look at the **U.S. Consumer Price Index** (published by the Bureau of Labor Statistics)[66] to understand long-term trends and economic shifts.

Core Common Denominator®

The *Core Common Denominator®* chart is a simple tool designed to help you evaluate where you are and then look ahead to where you want to go. You'll move through each of the four columns, taking time to be as thoughtful and thorough as possible. These columns include:

- Your loves or passions
- Your skills
- Your dreams and opportunities
- Your mission and purpose

If you want more space to reflect, expanded response pages are included in the bonus download that comes with this book.

Love	Skills	Opportunities	Purpose
Love to Do	Current Skills/ Experience	Dreams and Opportunities	Mission and Purpose
• Make sure some of these are artistic and recreational. • These should unlock the creative, or right side, of your brain. • Make the list extensive.	• These skills and experiences do not have to be recently used skills but things you know you are good at. • Draw from past experiences that may be lying dormant presently. • Include soft skills which can't be duplicated with artificial intelligence or a robot.	• How do you want to spend your day(s)? • If you could do anything you wanted, what would you do? Responses can include anything from donating your time to a worthy organization, starting your own business to helping an organization grow to its potential.	• This is your WHY? • What are you passionate about? What fuels you? How could you employ that passion to assist others and/or society?

Once you've worked through the chart, take a little extra time to think about what feels *possible* right now and what feels *out of reach*. Then, ask yourself: what steps could you take to reduce or even remove the things that seem impossible? You might be surprised at what starts to shift with a little intentional thought.

Explore the Possibilities

Feels Possible	⇄	Feels Impossible

_{DeborahJohnson}

In the next section, we'll look at how automation and tech tools can turn those "impossible" dreams into a much more "possible" reality.

PART FOUR

Create Your Automation Hub

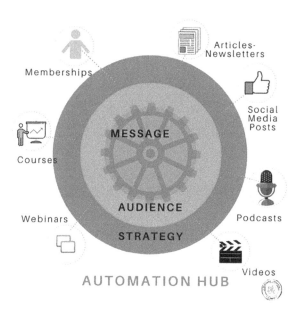

CHAPTER FIFTEEN

Creating a Content and Automation System

Thoughtful planning ensures that automation will enhance operations rather than create unnecessary complications.

I remember using a long metal rod to turn the old sprinkler valve on and off—something I don't miss at all. Now, our sprinklers are run automatically. At Christmas, our outdoor lights turn on at dusk and off after a set time, while landscape lights enhance our backyard every evening. Many home appliances, like heaters and air conditioners, are also programmable. Automation reduces the mental load of daily tasks, saving time and energy.

Making Automation Work for You

Implementing automation effectively requires a solid foundation on which to build. Just as installing a sprinkler system before laying sod leads to a muddy mess, automating a business without a strong base can cause inefficiencies. If landscape lights shine on dirt, the effect won't be the same as when they illuminate shrubs and trees placed strategically throughout the yard. In the same way, it's essential to establish clear products, services, and business fundamentals first before integrating automation tools. Thoughtful planning ensures that automation will enhance operations rather than create unnecessary complications.

Just as robotics streamline manufacturing by improving efficiency, automation in business can help manage tasks like customer communication, marketing, and content distribution. With a well-structured system, productivity increases, allowing more focus on higher-value work. Before automating, essentials like a website, value proposition, and business focus should be in place as automation works best when there's existing content and structure. However, AI tools can assist in creating these foundational elements with well-planned input and prompts. Once established, organizing a content bank for easy access further enhances efficiency. AI-driven automation for videos, voiceovers, and social media offers exciting possibilities for growth and creativity.

Over the years, I've created extensive content that I now store in an organized system, making it easily accessible for assistants anywhere in the world. A well-structured system creates freedom by streamlining workflow. In this section, I'll share tools that have been easy to automate. You'll find others that best fit your needs. My goal is to spark ideas that help you build a system tailored to your life and business.

The Importance of a Content Bank

In the financial world, a bank serves as a financial institution that provides a safe place for individuals and businesses to store, manage, and grow their money. The bank provides stability and protection of assets. It is also a place of transaction to gain access to stored resources.

Your content bank is a centralized place to store, manage, and grow your business assets, including graphics, photos, memes, videos and books. If this concept is new to you, start by assessing your existing content. Does it align with your current goals and messaging? Be intentional about creating or refining content to maintain clarity and avoid confusion. There's no need to rush, but don't hesitate to start or make changes. Growth comes from both successes and failures.

Begin by automating two key areas that enhance what's already working. This might be automating a social media account or starting a newsletter. Think of automation as a set of tools; then, add new ones gradually and with purpose, ensuring each serves a specific function, even if some overlap. Over time, your content bank will expand with additional articles, videos, and more. While new tools emerge constantly. This book will cover foundational principles and essential tools to help you get started.

Essential Tools for Business Automation

Password Management System

For years, I managed passwords by emailing a Word document to myself, constantly updating it—a system that was both outdated and insecure. Looking back, I now appreciate the value of a reliable password management system. Whether for personal use or business, having a secure, organized way to store and share passwords is essential. These systems are affordable and make it easy to grant access to trusted assistants without compromising security.

A good password manager not only stores credentials but also alerts you to weak, duplicate, or compromised passwords, allowing for quick updates to protect your accounts. When my website was hit by a major malware attack, my password system enabled my web team to swiftly change passwords while securing and cleaning up the site. With the growing threats of malware and ransomware, especially on platforms handling sensitive data, strong, encrypted passwords that are scrambled for security are no longer optional; they're a necessity.

Website

A website is essential for any business, serving as a digital business card and on your own real estate. Unlike social media platforms, where access and rules can change at any time, your website remains under your control. Think of it like owning a home versus renting. When you own, you set the rules, ensuring stability for your business presence. Having your main hub on your own domain provides long-term security and flexibility.

CHAPTER SIXTEEN

Building a Strong Online Presence

Learn enough to oversee the creation process and hire experts when desired or necessary.

There are many website-building options, and YouTube offers countless tutorials for guidance. I recommend using WordPress.org, the self-hosted version of WordPress, as it's cost-effective and highly customizable with free, open-source plugins. Plugins extend website functionality, adding features like SEO tools, security enhancements, and contact forms without altering the core site code. A web designer can help navigate these options and tailor the site to your needs.

However, be mindful that some plugins may conflict with others, causing functionality issues—a reason why having access to a trusted web team is valuable. Most hosting services offer domain registration and web hosting, both of which are necessary. Some even provide AI-driven tools to help with website creation, branding, email setup, and e-commerce integration, making it easier than ever for those who need technical support.

Website Essentials and Design

When I first launched my *DJWorksMusic* website, I hired a web design team to create a banner using code I didn't fully understand. I sketched and outlined page designs while paying for every addition and change, which quickly became expensive. Thankfully, those days are behind me. Today, website design has become much more accessible for entrepreneurs and do-it-yourselfers. However, not everyone wants to spend the time managing their own website design and updates.

While some AI programs can automate much of the website creation process, it's still helpful to learn the basics of web design. By doing so, you can take charge of managing your own content, usually with no knowledge of code. Many entrepreneurs now prefer making small changes to their websites themselves; with the right tools, it's easy. Even if you prefer not to handle the edits, I recommend learning enough to oversee the creation process and hire experts when necessary. It's also wise to have a trusted tech contact for support, as there will be times when you need help.

To set up a website, you need both a **domain name** (your website's address, like example.com) and **server space** (a subscription to storage on a server where your website's files live). Think of the **server** as the hub or home where all the parts of your website—text, images, code—are stored and managed, while the **domain** is the front door people use to find and access it. The server can host one or many domains, and subscribing to server space gives you the room to build and run your site.

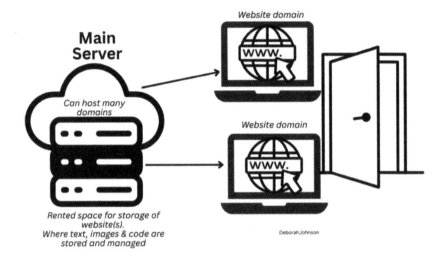

Making quick edits to a website without relying on an outside source is a huge convenience, though it depends on your confidence with the software. The need to learn code or design formats from scratch is gone, thanks to pre-made templates, easy-to-edit pages, and helpful instructional videos. Software providers want you to succeed, so they offer resources to guide you. For example, I use a WordPress plugin called *Thrive Architect*, which allows me to edit and view my website across all devices, ensuring it's mobile-friendly. Many other options are available to best fit your needs. Your website will never truly be "finished" as a content creator, so learning basic editing tools is crucial for making small updates efficiently.

Crafting a Clear Business Message

While creating a large, visually impressive website is appealing, the most important element is delivering a clear message and purpose, with a call to action. This should include a concise sentence supported by photos or illustrations that convey the message. Contact information and the call to action, whether it's an email link, sign-up form, or consultation button, should be easily accessible (see the book *Storybrand*[67] by Donald Miller for more ideas).

My biggest challenge has always been clarity. As someone who loves creativity, I naturally gravitate more towards cleverness rather than a simple message. But a clever message alone isn't always effective—like telling a joke that no one understands. On a website, that silence leads to inaction. Thus, your homepage should be clear, and once established, additional pages can be created to focus on specific aspects of the business or product. Content creation is crucial, especially for thought leaders and entrepreneurs. Blog articles, which are easy to format on most WordPress sites, don't need to be lengthy but should align with the website's main message. Long-form articles (1,000–3,000 words) help establish authority. These articles can also be repurposed in newsletters and other forms of content.

There are many resources available to develop articles, whether hiring a content creator, using AI tools for quick content generation, or self-publishing. It's vital to write in your authentic voice to maintain transparency. Afterward, editing with AI tools can refine the content, but all facts, especially statistics, must be verified with reliable sources to maintain credibility. AI-generated content can sometimes be inaccurate, so it's important to fact-check and ensure your information is trustworthy. If you include information that's not verifiable, it decreases trust in your brand and expertise.

Your website will evolve over time, so don't get stuck on perfection. You can scan multiple websites for ideas and inspiration but be authentic in creating your own voice and "story." As your business grows, you may create separate domains for different areas of focus, keeping them under the same server but directing customers to specific pages. For instance, I have distinct sites for my music and keynote speaking services, ensuring that each audience is directed to the right content. The music pages are fun pages with many videos, but it could be confusing and even distracting to someone looking for a speaker or online course. In fact, they may never get to my other products.

Growing and Managing a Mailing List

I've been sending a weekly newsletter for over 20 years. Even if people don't always read or open them, they recognize my name and expect my emails. That consistency keeps me on their radar. When you send regular updates, you remind your audience that you're still active. Early on, I used GoDaddy's basic email templates—bland and clunky. Now, e-marketing platforms offer beautifully designed templates that make creating emails much easier. There's a learning curve with any software, but most platforms have great resources to help you get up to speed quickly.

Building an email list should be your priority. Most platforms require a double opt-in to prevent spam complaints, and that's good. It ensures that people want to hear from you. One of the best ways to grow your list is by offering something valuable, like a free guide or exclusive content. Your email platform becomes your communication hub for sharing updates, insights, and offers. If you're "out of sight," you're often "out of mind," so staying visible is key.

I love that email marketing lets me repurpose content. If I publish an article on my website or LinkedIn, I'll include a short excerpt in my newsletter with a link to the full piece. This keeps emails concise while still providing value. I used to write long newsletters (too long, honestly), but I've learned that people appreciate quick takeaways with clear visuals. A great image and a few sentences can be enough to capture attention and direct readers to what interests them most.

Scheduling emails in advance has been a lifesaver, especially when I travel. I've had emails go out while I was in Africa, Italy, and Iceland—without worrying about a thing! It takes time to set up, but once scheduled, I can focus on other priorities like fun travel. I also use multiple lists to keep content relevant for different audiences, like goal setting, music, or speaking. A simple tip: always include your own email in each list for sending. This helps you catch formatting issues and broken links before your subscribers do.

There are plenty of e-marketing platforms, from those that have been around awhile like *Mailchimp, Constant Contact* and *AWeber* to newer options that may be more budget-friendly. Pricing is usually based on subscriber count, so keep an eye on costs. Some platforms offer lifetime deals, but do your research. If the service shuts down, moving your list can be a hassle. Always back up your email list so you're never at the mercy of a single platform. It is important to respect people's privacy. LinkedIn connections, for example, can't just be added to your email list unless they opt in. GDPR and other privacy laws matter, so always ask before adding someone. I usually send a quick message asking if they'd like to join, and the email platform takes care of the rest. Done right, email marketing is one of the easiest and most effective ways to automate your business and marketing while keeping that personal touch.

Writing Articles for Authority

You might wonder, *Why write articles when there's already so much information online? Is it worth the time?* or *How often should I publish?* These are all valid questions. In my experience, anyone looking to establish themselves as a thought leader should write. I publish articles as blog posts and include them in my newsletters; it's a great way to stay visible and share valuable insights. Years ago, someone suggested I get help with writing my weekly articles. At first, I felt a bit defensive, as if my work wasn't good enough. Writing didn't come naturally to me, and I was already battling my own doubts. However, I knew my content was solid, and more importantly, I was improving with every article. Looking back, I'm glad I didn't outsource everything. The process of writing consistently has made me a better communicator.

Over time, my short articles evolved into longer, more in-depth pieces as I became more comfortable with my messaging. I rewrote constantly, refining my ideas and learning what resonated with my audience. Writing books also pushed me to grow, especially when working with editors. Ultimately, nothing replaces the experience of writing regularly. The writing process becomes easier when you create a system for capturing ideas. So many great thoughts disappear simply because they're not documented. I'm not sure how many of my ideas are still floating around that I've not taken the time to document, just waiting to be grabbed! Keeping a simple note system—digital or on paper—ensures you always have material to work with.

One more thing: If you're writing, you should also be reading. Audiobooks count! Exposure to different writing styles, ideas, and perspectives make you a stronger writer. Warren Buffett (b.1930), multi-billionaire of Berkshire Hathaway, has credited his success in part to his intense reading habits—sometimes 500 to 1,000 pages a day in his younger years. That kind of input sharpens critical thinking and deepens knowledge. Even today, he reads extensively, focusing on financial reports, newspapers, and books to stay informed and make better investment decisions.[68]

If you're just starting a newsletter or blog, don't let it overwhelm you. A couple of well-thought-out paragraphs are enough to begin. AI tools have also become a fantastic resource. I often use them to refine sentences or spark new ideas. ChatGPT, Google, and Microsoft all offer free writing assistance as well as many e-marketing ideas and resources. With the right prompts, these tools can verify details and improve clarity. Just be sure to fact-check and follow up on all sources. Writing is a skill that develops over time, and with the right tools and habits, it gets easier—even enjoyable!

Creating Social Media Content Strategically

Creating social media content is easier than ever, thanks to creative tools—including AI. I've listed some of my go-to resources in the bonus download for this book as well as on my resource page, but new tools emerge constantly. The key is to choose what works best for you without getting lost in time-consuming technology. Your focus should remain on your core mission, not just on keeping up with every new tool.

Each social media platform has different content formats, including varying video sizes. Fortunately, many tools can easily adapt your existing content to fit these formats. With the rise of generative AI, creating fresh visuals or videos is now quicker and more efficient, requiring just a simple, very specific prompt.

If you have online courses, a newsletter, products, or a podcast, social media content should support and amplify them. Over time, your content library will grow, so having an organized system is essential. I use labeled folders and a master file on Google Drive to track everything, making it easy for my team to find and repurpose content. Google Sheets is my go-to for organization, allowing my virtual assistants to access and update information from anywhere in the world. A simple system like this can save time and streamline your workflow.

CHAPTER SEVENTEEN

Managing Digital Content Efficiently

Organizing your files properly from the start saves time in the long run.

Before diving into content creation for social media, it's smart to set up a reliable storage system. Cloud platforms like Dropbox and Google Drive offer dependable solutions. Your system should be easy to access—not just for you, but also for your assistant or team—while remaining secure and well-organized. I personally use Google Drive for everyday content storage because it's affordable and accessible for my virtual assistants worldwide.

Set it Up Right: Save Time Later

Organizing your files properly from the start saves time in the long run. Set up folders and subfolders to keep everything easy to find.

I also keep some folders private for personal notes and documents. Admittedly, I learned this the hard way. I initially created content without a solid system and had to reorganize later. But the good news? Much of my past content has remained useful, proving that a well-structured library can serve me well for years.

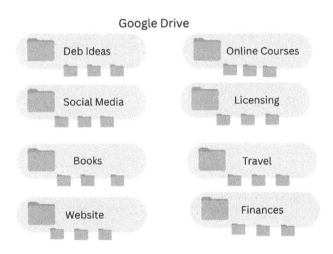

For larger files, like videos and audio for online courses, I use Amazon S3. It's highly secure and cost-effective for storing MP3s and videos. Each course page on my website is protected, ensuring only registered attendees can access the content. I also use Amazon S3 for lead magnets and free downloads, providing access through shared links. There is a learning curve when it comes to managing Amazon's storage buckets and permissions, but once you get the hang of it, it's a powerful tool and extremely cost-effective.

Because hard drives can fail unexpectedly (I've had a few quit on me!), I make sure all video and MP3 files are backed up both on separate hard drives and in the cloud. Each file is numbered, categorized, and documented in a Google Sheet with direct links for quick access. This simple system keeps everything organized and prevents future headaches.

If security is a concern, Amazon offers multi-factor authentication to prevent unauthorized access. Many large companies trust Amazon's cloud storage; as a small user, I've found it to be a reliable, long-term solution. Having a structured, secure system in place lets me focus on content creation with confidence.

Organizing a Creative Content Bank

Nearly everyone with a phone is already creating and posting content, but expanding a content bank strategically can make a big difference. When it comes to photos, there are plenty of copyright-free media sources, some available for free and others requiring a subscription or purchase. I use a mix of both. I also take my own photos when traveling, keeping folders of images that often come in handy. Surprisingly, I've used more of my own photos than I expected; plus, they serve as great reminders of past adventures.

For professional headshots and lifestyle images, I schedule a photo session every few years. These images are invaluable for podcasts, products, and marketing materials. Investing in quality photos has benefitted me, not just as an entertainer but also as a content creator. As a side note, a personal photo should be current and authentic enough that it does not surprise a client or audience who, by viewing the publicity photo, expects to meet a young, fit thirty-year-old but is shocked to encounter a much heavier fifty-something. The personal photo should match an individual's current appearance.

Tools like *Canva* offer access to graphics and stock photos, with usage rights depending on the subscription level. AI-powered design tools have also expanded, but their quality varies. Further, it's important to check copyright restrictions. Always do your homework; if a photo or logo requires permission, it's typically stated in a disclaimer. There are many free resources available, but it's crucial to read the fine print to avoid legal issues. For example, I once reviewed a book that contained a copyrighted logo that wasn't in the public domain. When I mentioned the logo in my review, the author wasn't happy. Not long after, I noticed Amazon removed the book from circulation, likely due to copyright infringement. This is a cautionary tale for content creators: using copyrighted material without permission can derail a project that took years to develop, and even worse, it could lead to legal action.

As a creator, I'm especially mindful of copyright since my work includes music, books, and trademarked products. While it's impossible to track every infringement, AI tools like YouTube's content detection system are getting better at flagging unauthorized use. I once had YouTube question one of my own songs simply because I had labeled it differently than its original album listing. Fortunately, I proved my ownership, but this highlights the growing complexities of AI, especially generative AI, in content protection.

AI-generated content exists in a legal gray area, and ongoing legislation will shape its ownership rules. While AI is a powerful tool for content creation, I still believe human creativity is unmatched. Even so, AI can be a great companion—helping to refine ideas, streamline workflows, and expand creative possibilities.

Structuring a Social Media System

Social media platforms like *LinkedIn, Facebook, Instagram, TikTok*, and *YouTube* are powerful tools for connecting with followers and promoting a brand. Consistently posting and maintaining a clear message can reduce the need for expensive ads. However, with so much content online, cutting through the noise is a challenge. While social media shouldn't replace a strong brand presence on a professional website, it's an essential part of a well-rounded marketing strategy.

Having a large following doesn't always translate to sales since likes and views fade quicker than a ten-minute burst of fame. However, tracking engagement helps identify what resonates with a particular audience. Over the years, I've developed a social media system that allows me to monitor weekly post performance and then, adjust as needed. My process has evolved, but the core structure remains the same. While I'll share what works for me, I encourage others to tailor a system that fits their needs.

My key tools include memes and videos in multiple formats, a content scheduler, and an organized filing system. In the beginning, I created content without a clear structure, which led to hours of searching for lost files. Eventually, I refined my system to make content easily accessible—not just for me, but also for my virtual assistants. While it's not perfect, it's efficient and saves time when onboarding help. The goal isn't perfection but getting started as "perfect is the enemy of done." It is important to build a system that works and refine it along the way. Whether someone is in her office or halfway around the world, having an organized process and system will keep her social media running smoothly. I've outlined the key elements of a simple system in the next section.

Using a Content Scheduler

I used to create a new, dated scheduling calendar every year, but I quickly realized that I didn't want to work that hard. Now, I use a week-specific calendar that allows for flexibility. When promoting a course or product, I ensure content is scheduled well in advance for maximum impact, and my virtual assistant knows exactly where to find it.

With a large content library, I rotate general, on-brand content throughout the year while noting outdated material that needs replacing. My VA handles these updates, keeping my content fresh without requiring me to start from scratch.

To streamline scheduling requires a scheduling tool. I used *Buffer* for years because it's affordable and works well for multiple platforms. Recently, I invested in a newer AI-driven tool with lifetime access, and I stick to the basics. Most schedulers require permission to link social media accounts, which is standard, but be wary of any platform asking for passwords. Also, automated posting is only available for public accounts, not personal Facebook pages.

Once linked, scheduling is simple. My VA typically schedules two weeks of content at a time, using my numbered memes and videos stored in Google Drive. Many schedulers now use AI to analyze past engagement and suggest optimal posting times, making it easier to reach the right audience. Some businesses hire marketing professionals or content creators, which can be a great time-saver. However, content styles vary widely, like flavors at an ice cream shop. Thus a business owner is responsible for ensuring all content aligns with his brand's vision.

Protecting Your Business Assets

Copyrights, trademarks, and patents each serve different purposes. While copyrights are relatively simple to obtain without legal assistance, trademarks and patents typically require an attorney. A copyright protects original works like books, music, and artwork, but not titles or short phrases. Trademarks, on the other hand, safeguard distinctive names, logos, and systems associated with a brand. For more in-depth guidance, numerous books, online tools, and videos provide step-by-step instructions on securing these protections.

Each year, more content enters the public domain, and online searches can help identify newly released works. However, copyright laws have evolved due to major companies pushing to extend protections, such as Disney. To check copyright status, visit *Copyright.gov*. The *Public Domain Information Project*[69] provides a list of public domain music while the *Harry Fox Agency* offers tools to obtain mechanical licenses for songs. Additional resources are available for researching copyright information on art, photos, and other media. There are also many subscription resources for licensing photos and music that are well-worth the investment.

Using Project Management Tools and Virtual Assistants

A project management tool is software designed to help teams plan, track and collaborate on projects by organizing tasks, deadlines, and resources effectively. For many businesses, these management tools improve their efficiency. The type of project management tool a business needs and the time required to implement it depends on the size and involvement of specific teams. However, having a system in place to track progress is essential.

Online tools like *Asana or Trello* have a free level that will work well for small teams. Start slowly, though, because the time it takes to implement different management programs can easily distract from the main work. It is important to pick something simple enough to keep your and your team organized and that you won't soon outgrow. Simple choices include Google docs and Excel sheets. They may work well for small teams, so don't discount them. Remember, there are new tools coming every day. Focus on the basic purpose of the tool; then, choose what will work best without a huge sacrifice of time. Simple is best.

Along with a management system, clear job descriptions should be provided for each assistant, particularly for roles that need to be filled. When I had to let a virtual assistant go unexpectedly, I found out the hard way that it is important to have an onboarding document. I had to backtrack to create a document and instructional videos, so I could easily onboard another assistant. Throughout this process, I found video works extremely well, especially with cultural, language and time differences. My new assistant could access a recorded video for most every part of a new process or task.

When outsourcing video editing of my podcast, I went through the same process of creating a training video. Because I like my podcast videos to be similar in style and do very little editing, I provide an additional document with a few timed cues for each video for my video editing team.

When hiring a virtual assistant (VA), it's important to clearly define what you're looking for—including the specific tasks, personality traits, and required skill level. For customer service, keep in mind that you usually get what you pay for. Great customer service and solid management can be the difference between making a sale or losing one. For example, when booking an international flight recently, I encountered two airlines offering similar flights at the same price. After multiple failed attempts to book online due to a server issue, I called one airline, only to be quoted a higher price than what was listed. Despite my showing proof of the online price, the representative refused to match it. So I immediately booked on the other airline. This experience was a strong reminder that clear communication, flexibility, and good management—whether in a small team or a large company—are essential to keeping customers.

CHAPTER EIGHTEEN

Leveraging Online Learning Platforms

Before investing time and resources into creating a course or membership platform, evaluate its purpose and potential engagement.

Online courses offer flexible, scalable learning opportunities that are accessible worldwide. They help individuals gain new skills and knowledge, but many courses go unfinished, with students often completing only 30% of the content. Before investing resources into creating a course or membership platform, it's important to evaluate its purpose and potential engagement. For instance, my first major course was based on my book *Stuck is Not a Four-Letter Word*. Initially, it featured eight long video segments with study guides, but I later reformatted it into sixty shorter videos with downloadable MP3s. This shorter format has proven more effective and is now my preferred approach for course creation.

The following sections outline key types of online hosting platforms and essential principles for membership sites. Understanding these options will help determine the best approach for one's e-learning goals.

Third Party e-Learning Platforms

Third-party e-learning platforms handle course hosting, payment processing, student access, and technical support. They provide a convenient way to launch online courses without managing the backend logistics. All course materials, including videos, MP3s, and downloads, are stored on the provider's website.

Platforms like *Udemy, Coursera, and Skillshare* have been hosting courses since 2010, acting as intermediaries between creators and students. When I first launched my music and professional development courses on Udemy, I appreciated their structured formatting guidance. They require the creator to provide a few free preview lessons to boost sales and demonstrate content quality. While course creators set their prices, the platform controls discounts, which can significantly cut into profits. Intellectual property remains with the creator, but students who purchase the course get lifetime access.

Losing control over pricing led me to transition from Udemy to self-hosting, but I gained valuable experience, positive reviews, and confidence in course creation. Other platforms like *Kajabi* offer course hosting for a monthly fee, often with built-in marketing tools. However, costs rise with multiple courses, and while setup is simplified with templates, there's still a learning curve. From experience, no course setup is truly "easy," but the reward of reaching a global audience makes the effort worthwhile.

With countless third-party platform options, choosing the right one depends on your goals. After testing different approaches, I ultimately opted for self-hosting to keep costs manageable and drive traffic to my website. The next section covers how I made that transition and what to consider when managing your own course platform.

Self-Hosted e-Learning Platforms

A self-hosted online course platform, or Learning Management System (LMS), allows individuals or organizations to create, manage, and deliver courses on their own servers. This gives full control over content, branding, and user data. However, large video and audio files require significant storage, which can become costly. Solutions like Amazon S3 or Dropbox store these files efficiently. Choosing the right platform is crucial since switching later is a lot of work. I've done it three times and learned the hard way! I've included recommended resources in the bonus download as well as my resource page to help you compare different options.

WordPress plugins like *LearnDash and WPCourseware* integrate with an existing site, allowing you to build courses within your website's theme. These plugins provide structured course layouts, and some include LMS templates. With the right website builder, such as *Thrive Themes or Elementor*, you can create a seamless learning experience. Videos and downloads are stored separately in your chosen storage system and linked privately within your course. WordPress also allows pages to be marked as "private," ensuring exclusive access for students.

After experimenting with multiple LMS platforms, I now host my courses on *Digital Access Pass* (DAP), a WordPress plugin originally designed for memberships and shopping carts. When DAP expanded to include a Learning Membership Platform, I moved my courses to that platform. This setup allows me to manage students, track progress, and integrate courses with membership programs—all in one place. I'm pleased with both the functionality and the professional look of my course pages.

If this technical talk seems overwhelming, don't worry. Start with the basics. Online courses and membership platforms go hand in hand, like peanut butter and jelly. New platforms emerge constantly, so research thoroughly and read honest user reviews. If you're just getting started, choose an affordable option that allows room for growth. Reliable customer support is also essential since you'll need it at some point! Above all, don't let fear hold you back. The lessons I've learned from my mistakes have been invaluable. I hope they help you avoid unnecessary frustration. Creating quality online courses takes effort, but a strong, purposeful message will fuel success.

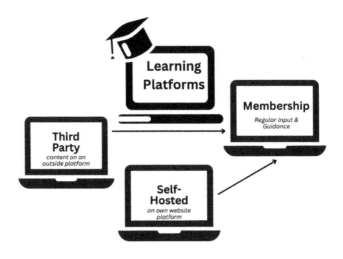

Membership Platforms for Recurring Revenue

Most course creators want students to engage with and complete their courses, but the reality is that many never even start. One solution is to provide structured guidance throughout the course. Adding mentorship or accountability features, as I've done in some of my courses, has significantly helped keep students on track with their goals. A membership platform creates a dedicated space for building community, fostering engagement, and delivering ongoing value. It allows businesses and creators to generate recurring revenue while offering members exclusive content, resources, and support. More than just access to material, it provides a sense of belonging and long-term value.

Many entrepreneurs successfully combine online courses with membership platforms by structuring regular engagement with attendees. Researching different formats and studying successful models can provide valuable insights. Some platforms offer tiered memberships, giving access to coaching or mastermind groups, while others incorporate quizzes and interactive elements to drive progress. The key is to encourage members not just to access content but to actively learn and grow. Incorporating accountability checkpoints, clear goals, and engagement strategies will help students succeed.

CHAPTER NINETEEN

Utilizing Video for Business Growth

*Choosing the right video platform
depends on your goals.*

In this section, I will explore various video platforms, including *YouTube, Vimeo,* and cloud-based storage systems like *Amazon S3* and *Dropbox*, highlighting their unique uses and key differences for content. Each platform offers distinct features tailored to different needs, whether it's YouTube's broad reach and searchability, Vimeo's professional and customizable presentation, or the secure, flexible hosting options provided by cloud storage systems. By understanding their strengths and limitations, you can select the best platform for your specific goals.

Choosing the Right Video and Storage Platform

Choosing the right video platform depends on your goals—whether it's maximizing reach, showcasing high-quality content, or securely storing videos. YouTube offers broad visibility and searchability, Vimeo provides a professional, ad-free viewing experience, and cloud-based storage platforms like Amazon S3 and Dropbox offer secure hosting for private content. Understanding the strengths and limitations of each will help determine the best fit for your needs. Many creators use a combination of these platforms to optimize their content strategy.

YouTube is a powerful tool for promotion and audience growth. As a Google-owned platform, it boosts SEO, expands reach, and allows videos to remain accessible long-term. Its shareable format increases visibility across multiple platforms, making it a great way to drive traffic and build brand recognition. YouTube also enables monetization through ads, though revenue is split, with creators receiving 55% and YouTube retaining 45%.

Setting up a YouTube channel is simple, even for beginners. Playlists help organize content and keep viewers engaged by automatically playing related videos. Years ago, I started using playlists for my music albums and have seen consistent growth in views. This feature not only improves user experience but also enhances watch time, increasing the likelihood of discovery by a broader audience.

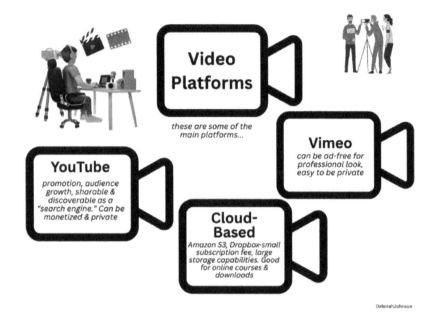

Vimeo offers a polished, ad-free environment ideal for professionals who want full creative control over their videos. Unlike YouTube, which prioritizes discoverability through search and ads, Vimeo focuses on privacy options, high-quality playback, and customizable embedding for websites. It's often preferred for portfolios, client presentations, or subscription-based content where presentation and exclusivity matter. It can also be used for protected online course videos.

Cloud-based Video is a great option for secure and flexible video hosting. Platforms like **Amazon S3** and **Dropbox** provide excellent solutions. Amazon S3 is highly scalable, offering customizable access controls and integration with other AWS tools, making it ideal for businesses with technical needs. Dropbox, on the other hand, is more user-friendly and works well for easy file sharing and collaboration. These platforms allow creators to retain full control over their content without relying on public video sites. There is a cost, but it is reasonable. I personally use Amazon S3 for online courses and licensing my music and MP3 downloads. I also use Dropbox for sharing some medium-sized video and audio files, especially for my podcast video editing team.

Establishing and Growing Your Video Channel

Every small business and entrepreneur should consider creating a YouTube channel to boost visibility—it's free promotion! You can personalize it with your logo and update it as needed. Focus on mastering the basics of posting with searchable topics and tags while staying informed with platform updates. Overall, develop a clear video strategy to keep content consistent and effective.

Creating video content has never been easier with smartphones and accessible tools like Zoom, which even offers a free plan. I have used a green screen for many videos but have also embraced a simple, consistent background for my podcasts and short videos. Having an easy, ready-to-go setup eliminates excuses and streamlines the production process.

For courses and product launches, I've invested in different backdrops, which are inexpensive and easy to hang in my office. Lighting, sound, and background setup are crucial, but without a Hollywood budget. YouTube offers a range of tutorials on video production tips. I even use portable banners as backdrops, which are both affordable and effective. Creating videos is like setting up a small movie set;

keeping it simple makes the process easier. Tech challenges are inevitable, and I've faced my share with different cameras, connections, and software compatibility issues. Some devices use USB, others HDMI, and I ended up using two separate laptops for recording—an unconventional solution, but it works!

Short-form videos (15-30 seconds) are also especially popular, qualifying for YouTube pre-roll and bumper ads. With AI-powered video creation tools, editing has become even easier, making professional-looking videos in multiple formats accessible to everyone, no technical expertise required.

CHAPTER TWENTY

Effective Lead Generation Strategies

Well-crafted lead magnets play a key role in marketing by attracting the right audience and capturing contact information for future engagement.

An effective lead generation strategy draws the right people to your business to build relationships right away. Whether it's through a free quiz, webinar, or a helpful PDF download, you're creating a first touchpoint that moves someone from being a cold contact to a warm lead. The goal? Build trust over time so that when they're ready to make a purchase, your product or brand is the one they think of first.

The Power of Lead Magnets

I've purchased some online courses because the creator provided enough valuable content upfront to earn my trust. I'm not easily sold, but lead magnets—like free PDFs, eBooks, templates, and videos—establish credibility and demonstrate expertise. These resources give potential customers a preview of the value a course or product can offer, making them more likely to invest. While much of the information in online courses can be found online or in PDF downloads for free, the organization, structure, and accountability that courses provide make them worth the investment.

Well-crafted lead magnets play a key role in marketing by attracting the right audience and capturing contact information for future engagement. By consistently offering valuable resources, businesses can build trust, grow their customer base, and increase conversion opportunities.

When creating a lead magnet, focus on what will add the most value for your ideal customer. Free downloads and webinars not only enhance marketing but also add a creative element to your business. One of my most popular downloads has been a side-business template—simple, fun, practical, and exactly what my target audience needs.

Hosting Webinars for Engagement

Hosting a free or low-cost webinar is a great way to build trust and establish expertise. Previously recorded webinars can easily be repurposed as lead magnets, making them a asset. When planning a webinar, choose a relevant topic and format that is accessible and engaging. If the quality is high and the content remains relevant over time, you can continue promoting it as an evergreen resource, which is a pre-recorded presentation that stays relevant, allowing access anytime. Unlike live webinars scheduled for specific dates, evergreen webinars are available on demand, giving viewers flexibility to engage at their convenience. Don't hesitate to share valuable content since it builds credibility in messaging and fosters trust with your audience.

Great webinar topics include in-depth eBooks on industry fundamentals, online courses teaching timeless skills, and software tutorials addressing ongoing user needs. I've used free webinars to introduce foundational concepts including mindsets and habits for more extensive online courses. They're an excellent addition to your content library and a smart way to nurture potential customers.

Launching a Podcast to Build Authority

The popularity of podcasts has exploded. I recently had a client who was anxious to launch a podcast, so I suggested she first produce at least eight episodes to establish a "podcast content bank." This way, her podcast will look like it has a track record of released episodes when the first episode is officially released. I told her to determine a podcast release schedule ahead of time that she could fulfill with consistency. By doing this advance work, she will be in the top 20% of those who start podcasts, as many, with good intentions, stop after the first ten to twelve episodes. Podcasts don't have to be weekly. They can be released twice a month or even once a month to start. You can increase the number of releases with bonus episodes or regular episodes after establishing a good foundation. I'm happy to say my client followed my advice and is doing well, building her audience and reach.

I was eager to produce a podcast, but I waited for the right time, one free of weighty responsibilities. For I was both president of a non-profit, and I was losing my father to cancer. The timing wasn't right for a podcast; nevertheless, I gathered ideas for topics and established a format. After almost two years of preparation, I fully launched my first episode; it proved to be a smart move. I had more clarity for my mission and could devote emotional energy to the show. Despite much production experience, I still learned a great deal about speaking to video, the interview process and how to curate topics most interesting to my audience. I have heard that the magic number of 300 repetitions is ideal for gaining expertise in a particular area. Looking back, after now producing more than 300 podcasts, I certainly feel more confident with my abilities.

A podcast is one of the quickest ways, besides a newsletter and articles, to establish expertise. An ideal podcast length is twenty to thirty minutes, but you can go for hours if you think your audience will listen! We've seen very popular podcasts like Joe Rogan hold an audience for three hours. However, he has high profile guests, and he's an expert at asking relevant questions. Also, he has the resources to support a research and tech team to help with production.

If producing a Podcast is in your future, start jotting down ideas for episodes now as it's not too early! You'll be amazed how handy and valuable that list will be. I cover a few of the technical details in the bonus material included with this book and have listed recording equipment I use on my resource page. There are many options for technical equipment, but I suggest sticking with basics that will help with choosing a microphone, hosting platform, and mastering.

My podcast is not only on multiple podcast channels, but also on a YouTube Podcast channel. Keep in mind that YouTube is more than just a video platform but also a powerful marketing tool, especially since it's owned by Google. I now have a team that helps me produce the videos, but I do provide specific instructions for additional graphics, a B-roll that advertises my content and a mastered MP3. Hiring out the entire process is easy, even for those not familiar with producing video. New AI tools are frequently released that can be helpful, but keep in mind that some may come with a steep learning curve.

There are producers who will do everything if you are willing to pay, but remember, a podcast must be sustainable. Most podcasts don't make money at first; they are a promotional tool. Ads can be implemented after reaching a certain number of downloads, but be aware that too many ads can be distracting. After producing a number of episodes, I started using my podcast topics for my weekly articles. With the advancement of podcast transcriptions and AI summaries, producing articles has become much easier. By establishing a workable system, these tasks won't be overwhelming. Here are some ideas of repurposing podcasts, some of which can be fulfilled by an assistant, including AI tools.

- Produce the podcast as an MP3 and as a video. *Zoom*, as other platforms, provides multiple media download options.

- Use an AI tool to extract at least two takeaways from the video for social media content in multiple formats.

- Write an article focusing on the main takeaways taken from the podcast. *Zoom* and other platforms provide not only transcripts but some also provide summaries.

- Create a couple podcast specific graphics in multiple formats for the episode and the article for social media posts and to include in newsletters.

- Create hashtags and a weekly social media release schedule. This can easily be fulfilled by a VA or inserting all content in a content scheduler.

CHAPTER TWENTY-ONE

Writing and Publishing Your Book

Evaluating the core message and marketability of a book is just as important as writing it.

P eggy Rowe's journey to becoming a published author is a testament to persistence. After facing rejections for six decades, she published her first book at age eighty, *About My Mother*.[70] The memoir, which humorously explores her relationship with her mother, quickly found an audience, selling 10,000 copies in just three weeks. Thanks in part to her son, Mike Rowe, sharing her work on social media, Peggy's storytelling reached a wide audience. Her story is proof that it's never too late to pursue a writing career.[71]

Using Books to Expand Your Brand

I love browsing bookstores, studying covers, titles, and bestseller lists to see what's capturing readers' attention. Airport bookstores, in particular, offer great insight since travelers often browse while waiting for flights. It may seem like every topic has been covered, and to some extent, that's true. But what hasn't been written is your unique perspective, shaped by your experiences and expertise.

You might wonder if writing a book is worth the effort, especially if it doesn't reach a wide audience. The return on investment isn't always measured in sales alone. While digital content is abundant, people still read books though studies indicate a decline in reading for pleasure. Factors like time constraints, social media, and mental health concerns play a role, but that hasn't stopped authors from publishing. Thanks to independent publishing, the process is more accessible than ever.

Bowker,[72] the U.S. agency that issues ISBNs, reported that self-published books surpassed one million ISBNs for the first time in 2017, with a major spike in 2019. Some traditionally published authors have even bought back their rights to self-publish, gaining more control over marketing and production. Regardless of the publishing path, most marketing responsibilities fall on the author unless a dedicated budget is in place. When teaching a college music business course, I reminded eager students that landing a record deal doesn't mean it comes with a big marketing budget. Most of the promotion still falls on the artist through touring and other efforts. Even with a budget, keeping an eye on spending is essential to maximize results.

With the average self-published book selling only 250 copies, writing a book should serve a greater purpose beyond sales. For many non-fiction authors, that purpose is establishing authority in their field. A book is also a great way to document original, trademarkable content. However, marketing remains the biggest challenge. That's why evaluating the core message and marketability of a book is just as important as writing it. Just a note—if you're tempted to let an AI tool write your entire book, please pause and rethink that idea. I've read and reviewed enough books to spot when a work was mostly generated by AI. Sure, it might *sound* polished and *look* decent, but often, it's bland and lacks uniqueness. Further, tools exist (including one Amazon uses for reviews) that can detect AI-generated content. Here's the bottom line: do the work. Write in your own voice. Use AI to help clarify or rephrase, not to replace your creativity.

Understanding Different Book Formats

eBooks

According to a 2023 article by *Wordsrated*, 30-34% of all ebooks sold are self-published.[73] The number of self-published books grew by 264% in the last five years. Partly this increase is due to the ease of their production. Amazon has made it easy to release books on their self-publishing platform, Kindle Direct Publishing. Producing an eBook version is essential in today's digital landscape, as it expands accessibility and reach to a global audience. The ebook provides readers with the convenience of instant downloads, adjustable text sizes, and compatibility across multiple devices, catering to different reading preferences. They also offer a cost-effective option for both authors and consumers to garner reviews that eliminates printing and distribution expenses while increasing potential sales.

Audiobooks

While the audiobook market is growing, many self-published authors hesitate to enter this market due to production costs. While it's possible to record your own audiobook, narrating it yourself is not for everyone. Hiring a professional narrator is an option, allowing for choices of gender, accent, and style. Audible, through its *ACX.com* platform, dominates the industry and offers both exclusive (40% royalties) and non-exclusive (25% royalties) distribution. Understanding these options can help you decide what works best.

I enjoy narrating my own books, and my office setup makes that possible. If you're considering it, do a test recording and get feedback. Many judge their voices too harshly. A pleasant, engaging tone is key. While rewarding, self-narration requires time, patience, and the right equipment, so be prepared if you choose to record your own book.

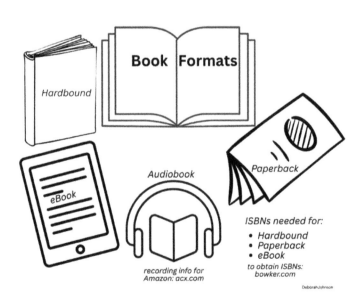

Print Books

Print books have existed for centuries. Even the stone tablets Moses used for inscribing the ten commandments contained print traditionally believed to date from c. 1446. After the Lord spoke to him on Mount Sinai in Exodus 20, God gave Moses two stone tablets inscribed by His fingers to be placed in the Ark of the Covenant (Exodus 31:18). These words as well as many other documents were so highly valued that scribes spent years making detailed copies, some of which archeologists have uncovered.

As an example of the importance of the written word, the Dead Sea Scrolls,[74] discovered between 1947 and 1956 in the Qumran Caves near the Dead Sea, comprise a collection of Jewish texts from the Second Temple period, which spans from approximately 516 BC to 70BC. Among these are numerous biblical manuscripts, representing some of the oldest known copies of texts from the Hebrew Bible. The scrolls include fragments from every book of the Hebrew Bible except Esther, with multiple copies of several books. For instance, there are 15 manuscripts of the Book of Genesis, 8 of Exodus, and 30 of Psalms. Notably, two nearly complete scrolls of the Book of Isaiah were found, providing invaluable insights into the textual transmission of this prophetic book.

Many other ancient texts have been meticulously copied over generations, allowing their knowledge and wisdom to endure, such as works from Aristotle (384-322 BCE). He wrote numerous works on philosophy, science, and politics.[75] The Nash Papyrus manuscript from 125 BCE, contains the Ten Commandments in Hebrew and was discovered over 100 years ago in Egypt.[76] This highlights the lasting significance of books and the written word, which have preserved history, culture, and ideas for centuries.

The written word remains highly valuable, particularly for those who create content and intellectual property. Many people also feel compelled to document their family history as a way to inspire and guide future generations. Writing memoirs serves as an excellent means to preserve these stories, ensuring they are passed down and remembered.

For print versions of your book, you should consider having it professionally formatted. The layout can include illustrations and photos with options for both hardbound and paperback versions. Most companies will provide examples of different chapter styles and text options. Some also provide additional services with editors and marketing opportunities for an extra fee. Since many options for formatting and printing exist, start this process early to gather resources and information. The company you hire to format your print version should also provide eBook formatting for an additional fee. It's important to obtain the correct format for your eBook to show up correctly on multiple devices as digital formats differ from the print version. You can proofread it as a PDF or ePub.

CHAPTER TWENTY-TWO

Closing Comments and Final Applications

We've walked through some tools and a simple system not only to identify your ideal lifestyle and work but also take practical steps toward making it a reality. New options are always popping up, and the ones you choose should come down to personal focus, the lifestyle you desire, and the system you put in place to support it. I can't say this enough: your uniqueness, your skillset, and your resources will truly set you apart from all the cookie-cutter options already available.

If It Sounds Too Good, It Might Be

Watch out for those "good deal" signups because they're not always as great as they sound. This applies to email marketing platforms too, especially if you're starting a newsletter. Be realistic about what you'll actually use and do your homework first. I try to choose programs that I won't quickly outgrow. When it makes sense, I'll go for lifetime access to skip the monthly or annual fees. Some subscription services sneak in extra charges as you grow so that more courses, more subscribers, means more money. With so many new tools popping up every day, there's no need to rush into anything. One of my go-to spots to explore software is *AppSumo*. They offer a satisfaction guarantee, which I've used more than once to return a tool that didn't fit my needs or was going to take too much time to implement. I always take time to read reviews and feedback before adding anything new to my toolbox.

How I Choose and Use New Virtual Tools

When I'm considering new software or virtual tools, I always start with research. I look for a clear return policy—because if the tool ends up being clunky or doesn't meet my needs, I want an easy way out. Simplicity and functionality are non-negotiables for me.

My Evaluation Process (Especially on Platforms Like *AppSumo*)

On sites like *AppSumo*, I dig into the reviews. I look for consistent feedback—if several users complain about a confusing interface or poor customer support, that's a warning sign. I also factor in that many of these tools come from emerging companies. There's some risk—they may not stick around long-term—but there's also high reward: many are rapidly evolving and offer lifetime deals that can be fantastic value.

Example: Video and Livestreaming

While comparing a new video/livestreaming platform to Zoom—the current standard thanks to its rise during COVID—I took a few extra steps:

- I visited the tool's website to watch demo videos and tutorials.
- I emailed support with specific questions (like whether recordings could be paused during podcast interviews and if it had a waiting room feature). While the answers were "not yet," the tool did offer strong multichannel livestreaming, which was a major plus.
- Best of all, I had 60 days to try it out risk-free—AppSumo is excellent with returns.

Testing and Making a Decision

There was a learning curve, especially streaming to LinkedIn, and I did have to contact support more than once. But ultimately, I chose to keep it. The company had two years of funding secured, which reassured me about its stability. I won't pay anything more, and I believe the tool's value will increase as its features improve—making it a smart long-term investment.

Reflection and Next Steps

Not long ago, I had to take my own advice, by asking myself, what makes me unique? When creating media for my online presentations, I was slipping into the trap of conformity, making my content look like everyone else's. As a shortcut, I had been following someone else's blueprint without fully tailoring it to my own strengths. Consequently, I used my skills to add more spark, more personality, and uniqueness so that I could better engage people and apply what I was teaching. Here is the lesson: just like me, you are unique, so do not lose sight of your uniqueness. Your gifts, your messages set you apart from others. So take time to uncover your value; own it, and actually use it. Once you've nailed down your unique selling proposition and clearly defined your audience, you'll feel a fresh sense of confidence, clarity, and momentum. That's what I want for you—a business and lifestyle you truly own, instead of one that owns you.

Applying What You've Learned

Take the time to make notes and comments for each of these areas. They are also listed and expanded in the bonus content included with this book.

- Assessment: HALFERS Tool™
- Assessment: Core Common Denominator®
- Assessment: Core Values
- A Lifestyle that Aligns with Your Values
- Creating a Content Bank
- Setting up Automation and Posting System
- Clear Messaging through a Website
- Setting up a Storage System
- Project Management System
- Online Learning and Membership Platforms Decisions
- Using Video Platforms
- Creating Lead Magnets
- Launching a Podcast
- Publishing Books

Quotes

Once there is a simple understanding of the basic way AI works, the fear will disintegrate.

Think of AI as an opportunity to grow and innovate at your own pace.

The possibilities for AI applications span nearly every industry, offering transformative potential.

Strike a balance between the freedom you long for and the fulfillment that comes from using your expertise to make a difference and give back.

The "What ifs" can spark hope, inspiring you to dream, to act and to believe in possibilities yet to come.

Neuroplasticity empowers individuals like you and I to view capabilities not as fixed entities but as dynamic and expandable potentials.

A well-defined mission serves as a guiding star in business.

Mental discipline is just as crucial as physical repetition in mastering any craft.

A clear and unique "Why" creates focus and resilience.

Discovering your core passion not only explains past career choices but also shapes future directions.

History shows that businesses able to adapt tend to succeed in tough times.

Understanding the distinction between appreciating and depreciating assets helps guide smarter financial and creative decisions.

Thoughtful planning ensures that automation will enhance operations rather than create unnecessary complications.

Learn enough to oversee the creation process and hire experts when desired or necessary.

Organizing your files properly from the start saves time in the long run.

Before investing time and resources into creating a course or membership platform, evaluate its purpose and potential engagement.

Choosing the right video platform depends on your goals.

Well-crafted lead magnets play a key role in marketing by attracting the right audience and capturing contact information for future engagement.

Evaluating the core message and marketability of a book is just as important as writing it.

About the Author

Deborah Johnson, M.A., is an accomplished author, speaker, composer, and entertainer. *Power of After* is her seventh book, adding to a long list of major creative projects. She has released multiple music albums, written hundreds of songs, and composed three full-length musicals. Deborah also hosts the popular podcast *Women at Halftime*, which explores mid-career transitions and navigating the halftime stage of life.

A lifelong creator, Deborah is energized by the creative process and finds deep fulfillment in teaching. She is especially inspired when her work helps others overcome fear and self-limiting beliefs.

In addition to writing and creating, she enjoys the outdoors and often plans active getaways with her husband, a former professional athlete, to stay active and inspired. Her children and grandchildren are a constant source of joy and remain one of her top priorities.

Up for multiple GRAMMY Award® nominations and spending over two decades in the entertainment industry, Deborah has also built several successful self-driven businesses. She continues to speak and perform at both live and virtual events, using her unique blend of talents to help others maximize their skills, experiences, and resources for meaningful impact.

Resources

These are some of Deborah's online resources for professional and personal development as well as music. If you are not receiving her weekly updates, it's free to sign up. She consistently shares many free resources in her newsletter as well as weekly articles and podcasts. Your information is never shared. Subscribers can opt out at any time. (but rarely do!)

Weekly updates with articles, videos and downloads:
https://GoalsForYourLife.com/newsletter

Podcast:
https://WomenatHalftime.com

Resources:
https://GoalsForYourLife.com/resources

Speaking Topics:
https://DeborahJohnsonSpeaker.com

Free Downloads:
https://GoalsForYourLife.com/DJWorks

Books and Products:
https://GoalsForYourLife.com/goal-setting-products/

Signature course with elite mentorship:
https://HeroMountainSummit.com

Music Albums and Products:
https://DJWorksMusic.com/products

Sheet Music:
https://DJWorksMusic.com/sheet-music

Musicals:
https://DJWorksMusic.com/musicals

Bonus Material

Power of After downloads:
https://GoalsForYourLife.com/powerofafterdownloads

We love hearing from our readers—your reviews not only encourage us but also help others discover meaningful and inspiring books they might otherwise miss. Thank you for sharing your thoughts!

Endnotes

1. *"How Many New Websites are Created Daily?"* Oddball Marketing, accessed April 7, 2025, *https://oddballmarketing.com.au/blog/how-many-new-websites-are-created-daily/*

2. Bernard Marr, "How Much Data Do We Create Every Day? The Mind-Blowing Stats Everyone Should Read," Forbes.com, May 21, 2018/accessed April 7, 2025, *https://www.forbes.com/sites/bernard-marr/2018/05/21/how-much-data-do-we-create-every-day-the-mind-blowing-stats-everyone-should-read/*

3. Scott McNutt, *"Happy Global Business Analysis Day—Do You Know What Your Business Data is Doing?"* Haslam College of Business, November 1, 2022/accessed April 7, 2025, *https://haslam.utk.edu/news/happy-global-business-analysis-day-do-you-know-what-your-business-data-is-doing/*

4. Tong Wu, Eric Lucas, Fanghui Zhao, Partha Basu, Youlin Qiao, *"Artificial Intelligence Strengthens Cervical Cancer Screening—Present and Future,"* Cancer Biology & Medicine, September 2024/accessed April 8, 2025, *https://www.cancerbiomed.org/content/early/2024/09/19/j.issn.2095-3941.2024.0198*

5. American Cancer Society medical and editorial content team, *"Key Statistics for Cervical Cancer,"* American Cancer Society, January 16, 2025/accessed April 8, 2025, *https://www.cancer.org/cancer/types/cervical-cancer/about/key-statistics.html*

6. Melissa Rudy, *"Woman says ChatGPT saved her life by helping detect cancer, which doctors missed,"* April 24, 2025/accessed May 2, 2025, https://www.foxnews.com/health/woman-says-chatgpt-saved-her-life-helping-detect-cancer-which-doctors-missed

7. Paypal team, *"Fraud Protection,"* Paypal Developer, August 15, 2024/accessed April 8, 2025, https://developer.paypal.com/docs/checkout/advanced/customize/fraud-protection/

8. Sam Ransbotham, Shervin Khodabandeh, *"How a 160-Year-Old Startup Uses AI: The Heineken Company's Ronald den Elzen,"* interview of Ronald den Elzen, on Me, Myself and I, MIT Sloan Management Review, January 7, 2025/accessed April 8, 2025, https://sloanreview.mit.edu/audio/how-a-160-year-old-startup-uses-ai-the-heineken-companys-ronald-den-elzen/

9. https://chatgpt.com/

10. *"Aristotle"* World History Encyclopedia, access April 14, 2025, https://www.worldhistory.org/timeline/aristotle/.

11. Pope John Paul II, *"Laborem Exercens,"* August 19, 2012/access April 12, 2025, https://justmecatholicfaith.wordpress.com/2012/08/19/laborem-exercens/

12. Melanie Espeland, *"The ROI of Executive Coaching: A Comprehensive Guide,"* Forbes, February 24, 2023/accessed April 8, 2025, https://www.forbes.com/councils/forbescoachescouncil/2023/02/24/the-roi-of-executive-coaching-a-comprehensive-guide/

13. Michael Sheetz, *"Elon Musk wants SpaceX to Reach Mars so humanity is not a 'single planet species,'"* CNBC, April 23, 2021/accessed April 8, 2025, https://www.cnbc.com/2021/04/23/elon-musk-aiming-for-mars-so-humanity-is-not-a-single-planet-species.html.

14. Stuart Jeffries, *"Chris Hoy: 'I had no natural ability as a cyclist!'"* The Guardian, October 2020/accessed April 8, 2025, https://www.theguardian.com/books/2020/oct/20/chris-hoy-natural-ability-cyclist-be-amazing-olympic-beyonce.

15. Geico Editorial Team, "Leo and Lillian Goodwin: American Dreamers." Geico, accessed April 8, 2025, https://www.geico.com/about/corporate/history-the-full-story/.

16 Peter T. Paul College of Business and Economics, *"Harland 'Colonel' Sanders,"* University of New Hampshire, accessed April 8, 2025, *https://paulcollege.unh.edu/rosenberg/pioneers/harland-colonel-sanders.*

17 Ben Boyd, *"Peloton Reintroduces Itself for Anyone, Anywhere,"* Peloton, May 23, 2023/accessed April 8, 2025, *https://investor.onepeloton.com/news-releases/news-release-details/peloton-reintroduces-itself-anyone-anywhere.*

18 Editorial Team, "Nokia Marketing Strategy 2025: A Case Study," The Big Marketing, accessed April 8, 2025, *https://thebigmarketing.com/nokia-marketing-strategy/.*

19 Deborah Johnson, *Stop Circling: Steps to Escape Endless Roundabouts,* (2023), 133-141.

20 Jeffrey A. Trachtenberg, *"Sales of Bibles are Booming, Fueled by First-Time Buyers and New Versions,"* The Wall Street Journal, December 1, 2024/accessed April 8, 2025, *https://www.wsj.com/business/media/sales-of-bibles-are-booming-fueled-by-first-time-buyers-and-new-versions-d402460e.*

21 Deborah Johnson, *Bad Code: Overcoming Bad Mental Code that Sabotages Your Life,* (2016), 129-130.

22 Matt Puderbaugh, Prabhu D. Emmady, "Neuroplasticity," National Library of Medicine, May 1, 2023/accessed April 8, 2025, *https://www.ncbi.nlm.nih.gov/books/NBK557811/.*

23 Harrison Wein, PhD., editor, *"Good Sleep for Good Health,"* News in Health, April 2021/accessed April 8, 2025, *https://newsinhealth.nih.gov/2021/04/good-sleep-good-health.*

24 Johnson, *Stop Circling,* 92-105.

25 B.R. Nanda, "Mahatma Gandi," Britannica, April 1, 2025/accessed April 8, 2025, *https://www.britannica.com/biography/Mahatma-Gandhi.*

26 *"Nelson Mandela,"* Wikipedia, accessed April 8, 2025, *https://en.wikipedia.org/wiki/Nelson_Mandela*

27 "Londolozi Private Game Reserve," *https://www.londolozi.com/.*

28 Sarah DeSantis, *"Imposter Syndrome: We All Feel Like a Fraud Sometimes,"* The Psychology Group, accessed April 8, 2025, *https://thepsychologygroup.com/imposter-syndrome/*.

29 Ariana Brockington, "Tom Hanks Opens Up About Having Imposter Sydrome around Paul Newman," Yahoo! News, September 5, 2022/accessed April 8, 2025, *https://www.yahoo.com/news/tom-hanks-opens-having-imposter-015600999.html*.

30 Johnson, *Bad Code*.

31 Majority Staff Report, *"A 'Kill Chain' Analysis of the 2013 Target Data Breach,"* Committee on Commerce, Science and Transportation, March 26, 2014/accessed April 8, 2025, *https://www.commerce.senate.gov/services/files/24d3c229-4f2f-405d-b8db-a3a67f183883*.

32 Amy Shira Teitel, *"What Caused the Challenger Disaster?"* History, March 5, 2025/accessed April 8, 2025, *https://www.history.com/articles/how-the-challenger-disaster-changed-nasa*.

33 "Biography," Jascha Heifetz, accessed April 8, 2025, *https://jaschaheifetz.com/about/biography/*.

34 Ayke Agus, *Heifetz As I Knew Him*, (Amadeus, 2005).

35 "Cultural Icon," Kodak Company, accessed April 8, 2025, *https://www.kodak.com/en/company/page/history/*.

36 Michael Zhang, *"What Kodak Said About Digital Photography in 1975,"* PetaPixel, September 21, 2017/accessed April 8, 2025, *https://petapixel.com/2017/09/21/kodak-said-digital-photography-1975/*.

37 Transcript, *"21 Seeds: Kat Hantas,"* Podcast World, October 21, 2024/accessed April 8, 2025, *https://www.podcastworld.io/episodes/21-seeds-kat-hantas-eg5gfv3d*.

38 Cal Newport, *So Good They Can't Ignore You: Why Skills Trump Passion in the Quest for Work You Love*, (Grand Central Publishing, 2012)

39 "Thomas Edison Quotes," Charles Edison Fund, accessed April 8, 2025, *https://www.charlesedisonfund.org/edison-quotes-images*.

40 "Hal David: 2012 Gershwin Prize Winner," Library of Congress, accessed April 8, 2025, *https://www.loc.gov/item/n80050146/hal-david/*.

41 Transcript, *"21 Seeds: Kat Hantas,"* Podcast World

42 Raquel Welch, *Raquel: Raquel Welch Total Beauty and Fitness Programme*, (Henry Holt & Co, 1987)

43 Naz Beheshti, *"5 of the Most In-Demand Soft Skills Companies Are Looking For This Year,"* January 28, 2020/accessed May 2, 2025, *https://www.forbes.com/sites/nazbeheshti/2020/01/28/5-of-the-most-in-demand-soft-skills-companies-are-looking-for-this-year/*

44 Dan Brodnitz, *"The Most In-Demand Skills for 2024,"* LinkedIn Talent Blog, February 8, 2024/accessed April 8, 2025, *https://www.linkedin.com/business/talent/blog/talent-strategy/linkedin-most-in-demand-hard-and-soft-skills.*

45 Tom Oliver, *"From Boom to Bust: Learning from Famous Family Business Failures,"* Inquirer.net, September 4, 2023/accessed April 8, 2025, *https://business.inquirer.net/419008/from-boom-to-bust-learning-from-famous-family-business-failures.*

46 Emil Persson, *"The LEGO Story: Building a Business Brick by Brick,"* Quartr, May 2, 2024/accessed April 8, 2025, *https://quartr.com/insights/company-research/the-lego-story-building-a-business-brick-by-brick.*

47 *"Infomercial Products, but they get increasingly more outrageous,"* YouTube Video, 19:02, Cohen Thompson, June 4, 2024, *https://youtu.be/cmOX_q6ncsg?si=guH6fJ1Ai0vVq-Io* .

48 Sean Everett, *"How Febreze's Marketing Genius Can Save Your Startup,"* Humanizing Tech-Medium, December 12, 2016/accessed April 8, 2025, *https://humanizing.tech/how-febrezes-marketing-genius-can-save-your-startup-c4bdfdab4710.*

49 *"Elton John claims Bach and Beethoven are his influences,"* Classic FM, October 28, 2013/accessed April 8, 2025, *https://www.classicfm.com/composers/bach/news/elton-john-bach-beethoven-influences/.*

50 Dorothy Hernandez, *"How a West Bloomfield Student Founded a Successful Business—at age 9,"* Second Wave Media, February 21, 2018/accessed April 8, 2025, *https://www.secondwavemedia.com/metromode/features/zollipops.aspx.*

51 Olivia Stringer, *"I quit uni to pursue my childhood side hustle full time—now it makes £256k a year, it was the best decision I ever made,"* The Sun UK, August 11, 2024/accessed April 8, 2025, https://www.thesun.co.uk/fabulous/29818337/side-hustle-business-success-money/.

52 Jack Zenger, Joseph Folkman, *"Research: Women Score Higher Than Men in Most Leadership Skills,"* Harvard Business Review, June 25, 2019/accessed April 8, 2025, https://hbr.org/2019/06/research-women-score-higher-than-men-in-most-leadership-skills.

53 Larisa Brown, *"The geek who builds lethal AI weapons, with a hotline to Trump,"* The Times, February 27, 2025/accessed April 12, 2025, https://www.thetimes.com/uk/defence/article/palmer-lucky-ai-billionaire-oculus-vr-dive-pjf20qktj

54 Jeremy Stern, "From Virtual Reality to Remaking our Bloated Defense Industry, Palmer Luckey is Trying to Forge a New America. Will it Let Him?" Tablet Mag, August 2024/accessed April 8, 2025, https://www.tabletmag.com/feature/american-vulcan-palmer-luckey-anduril.

55 Newport, *So Good they Can't Ignore You*

56 Maslow, A. H. (1943). *A Theory of Human Motivation*. Psychological Review, 50(4), 370–396.

57 Jennifer Herrity, *"Maslow's Hierarchy of Needs: Applying it in the Workplace,"* Indeed, January 28, 2025/accessed April 8, 2025, https://www.indeed.com/career-advice/career-development/maslows-hierarchy-of-needs.

58 *"Cosmetic & Beauty Products Manufacturing in the US—Number of Businesses (2002-2031),"* February 2025/accessed April 8, 2025, https://www.ibisworld.com/united-states/number-of-businesses/cosmetic-beauty-products-manufacturing/499/.

59 Donald Miller, *Building a Storybrand 2.0: Clarify Your Message So Customers will Listen*, (Harper Collins Leadership, January 7, 2025)

60 Dave Roos, *"10 Recession-proof Businesses,"* Money, accessed April 8, 2025, https://money.howstuffworks.com/10-recession-proof-businesses.htm.

61 Robert B. Waltz and David G. Engle, "The Ballad Index," Copyright 2025/accessed May 2, 2025, *https://balladindex.org/Ballads/K356.html*.

62 Adam McCann, *"Average Credit Card Debt,"* WalletHub, April 8, 2025/accessed April 8, 2025, *https://wallethub.com/edu/cc/average-credit-card-debt/25533*.

63 Jorge Martinez, *"29 Credit Card Debt Statistics for 2025 That You Should Know,"* DocuClipper, March 17, 2025/accessed April 8, 2025, *https://www.docuclipper.com/blog/credit-card-debt-statistics/*.

64 Deborah Johnson, *Stuck is Not a Four-Letter Word: Seven Steps to Getting Un-Stuck*, (iUniverse, 2013), 175-184.

65 Lauren Schwahn, "Free Budget Template and Tips for Getting Started," Nerdwallet, April 7, 2025/accessed April 8, 2025, *https://www.nerdwallet.com/article/finance/budget-worksheet*.

66 U.S. Bureau of Labor Statistics, "Consumer Price Index," *https://www.bls.gov/cpi/*

67 Miller, *Storybrand*

68 Marcel Schwantes, *"In a Few Words, Warren Buffet Reminds us of a Forgotten Habit that Led to His Success,"* Inc, November 8, 2021/accessed April 8, 2025, *https://www.inc.com/marcel-schwantes/in-a-few-words-warren-buffett-reminds-us-of-a-forgotten-habit-that-led-to-his-success.html*.

69 *Public Domain Music, https://www.pdinfo.com/*.

70 Peggy Rowe, *About My Mother: True Stories of a Horse-Crazy Daughter and her Baseball-Obsessed Mother*, (Forefront Books, 2023)

71 *"Peggy Rowe,"* Forefront Books, accessed April 8, 2025.

72 Jim Milliot, *"Self-Publishing is Thriving, According to Bowker Report,"* Publishers Weekly, February 17, 2023, accessed April 8, 2025, *https://www.publishersweekly.com/pw/by-topic/industry-news/publisher-news/article/91574-self-publishing-is-thriving-according-to-bowker-report.html*.

73 Nicholas Rizzo, *"Self-Published Books & Author Sales Statistics [2023],"* January 30, 2023/accessed April 8, 2025, *https://wordsrated.com/self-published-book-sales-statistics/*.

74 "List of the Dead Sea Scrolls," *https://en.wikipedia.org/wiki/List_of_the_Dead_Sea_Scrolls*.

75 Joshua J. Mark, *"Aristotle,"* WorldHistory.org, May 22, 2019/accessed April 8, 2025, *https://www.worldhistory.org/aristotle/*.

76 Somapika, *"6 Oldest Manuscript in the World,"* Oldest.org, March 26, 2025/accessed April 8, 2025, *https://www.oldest.org/culture/manuscript/*.

www.ingramcontent.com/pod-product-compliance
Lightning Source LLC
LaVergne TN
LVHW072146260725
817159LV00015B/194